# Soundings

*Issue 33*

# Convivial Cultures

FOUNDING EDITORS
Stuart Hall
Doreen Massey
Michael Rustin

EDITOR
Jonathan Rutherford

MANAGING EDITOR
Sally Davison

ASSOCIATE EDITORS
Geoff Andrews
Sarah Benton

REVIEWS EDITOR
Jo Littler

ART EDITOR
Tim Davison

EDITORIAL OFFICE
Lawrence & Wishart
99a Wallis Road
London E9 5LN

ADVERTISEMENTS
Write for information to
Soundings,
c/o Lawrence & Wishart

SUBSCRIPTIONS
2006 subscription rates are (for three issues):
UK: Institutions £80, Individuals £35
Rest of the world: Institutions £90, Individuals £45

Collection as a whole © Soundings 2006
Individual articles © the authors 2006
Cover photo © Vanessa Winship

No article may be reproduced or transmitted by any means, electronic or mechanical, including photocopying, recording or any information storage and retrieval system, without the permission in writing of the publisher, editor or author

ISSN    1362 6620
ISBN    1-905007-45-0

Printed in Great Britain by
Cambridge University Press, Cambridge

Soundings is published three times a year, in autumn, spring and summer by:
Lawrence & Wishart,
99a Wallis Road, London E9 5LN.
Email: soundings@lwbks.co.uk

**Website: www.lwbooks.co.uk/journals/soundings/contents.html**

# CONTENTS

**Editorial** 7
Sally Davison

**Commentary: A wonderful life** 9
Jonathan Rutherford

**Living in utopia** 13
Zygmunt Bauman

**Fear of difference/ fear of sameness:** 24
**the road to conviviality**
Roshi Naidoo

**For the sake of argument: re-imagining** 34
**political communication**
Alan Finlayson

**The power of play** 44
Pat Kane

**Musical jihad** 57
Amir Saeed

**Late capitalist nights** 66
Jonathan Keane

**Living inferiority** 76
Simon J. Charlesworth, Paul Gilfillan, Richard Wilkinson

**Prisons and how to get rid of them** 89
David Wilson

**The Mothers of May Square** 100
Richard Minns

**Westward look, the land is bright: race and** 106
**politics in the Andes**
Richard Gott

*Continued on next page*

*Soundings*

*Continued from previous page*

**Eurasia at the crossroads** 119
*Christoph Bluth*

**Three poems** 131
*Al-Saddiq Al-Raddi, Medbh McGuckian, Michael Longley*

**Detente at the Flying Horse** 139
*Barry Gifford*

**Reviews** 143
*John Jordan, Jeremy Gilbert*

**Feminism and economics** 151
*Sue Himmelweit*

**Labour must die** 163
*Andy Pearmain*

# NOTES ON CONTRIBUTORS

**Zygmunt Bauman** is Emeritus Professor of Sociology at the University of Leeds, and the author of numerous books and essays on philosophy and modernity.

**Christoph Bluth** is Professor of International Studies at the University of Leeds. His most recent publication is *The Nuclear Challenge*, Ashgate 2000.

**Simon J. Charlesworth** is the author of *A Phenomenology of Working-Class Experience*, Cambridge University Press 2000.

**Alan Finlayson** is a Senior Lecturer in the Department of Politics and International Relations, Swansea University. Recent publications include *Making Sense of New Labour*, Lawrence & Wishart 2003; and *Contemporary Political Theory: A Reader and Guide*, Edinburgh University Press 2004.

**Mark Ford** has published two collections of poetry, *Landlocked*, Chatto & Windus 1992; and *Soft Sift*, Harcourt Brace 2003. He has also edited two collections of the poetry of the New York School, *The New York Poets I*, Carcanet 2004; and *The New York Poets II* (with Trevor Winkfield) Carcanet 2005.

**Barry Gifford**'s novels have been translated into twenty-seven languages. He was co-author with David Lynch of *Lost Highway* (1997), and Lynch's film *Wild at Heart* was based on his novel. His most recent books include *The Phantom Father*, a New York Times Notable Book of the Year, and *Wyoming*, a Los Angeles Times Novel of the Year. www.BarryGifford.com.

**Jeremy Gilbert** teaches Cultural Studies at the University of East London. His latest book, *Anticapitalism: Popular Politics and Cultural Theory*, will be published by Berg.

**Paul Gilfillan** studied for his PhD at Edinburgh University.

**Sue Himmelweit** is a Professor of Economics at the Open University.

**Richard Gott**, once *The Guardian's* correspondent in Latin America, is the author of *Cuba: A New History*, Yale University Press 2004, and of *Hugo Chavez and the Bolivarian Revolution*, Verso 2005.

**John Jordan** spends his time trying to dismantle capitalism using myriad forms of creative resistance. He is co-editor of *We Are Everywhere: The Irresistible Rise of Global Anticapitalism*, published by Verso.

**Pat Kane** is a writer, musician, consultant and activist. He is the author of *The Play Ethic: A Manifesto for a Different Way of Living* (Macmillan 2004), a Visiting Fellow at the School of Management, University of York, partner in the New Integrity consultancy, and one-half of the soul-jazz duo Hue and Cry.

**Jonathan Keane** is a writer and arts programmer. For the past four years he has worked as senior programmer for the London Lesbian and Gay Film Festival. He has also had a year stint as Artistic Director for queerupnorth International Festival in Manchester. He has written for *Attitude*, *Fable* and *Upstart* magazines, and a wide range of other publications.

**Hafiz Kheir** was born in Khartoum, Sudan. He is a writer, translator and filmmaker. He has written and published poems, short stories and articles on media, the arts and language in various Arabic newspapers and magazines, as well as in Sudanese publications. He is now based in London.

**Michael Longley** has published eight collections of poetry including *Gorse Fires* (1991), which won the Whitbread Poetry Award, *The Ghost*

*Orchid* (1995) and *The Weather in Japan* (2000) - which won the Hawthornden Prize, the T. S. Eliot Prize and the Irish Times Poetry Prize. His most recent collection is *Snow Water* (2004). His *Collected Poems* will be published in 2006/7. He lives and works in Belfast.

**Roshi Naidoo** is a freelance researcher specialising in cultural politics for the heritage sector. She has co-edited (with Jo Littler) *The Politics of Heritage: the legacies of 'race'*, Routledge 2005.

**Medbh McGuckian** teaches Creative Writing at the Seamus Heaney Poetry Centre, Queen's University, Belfast. Her latest collection is *The Book of the Angel* (2004). She was awarded the 2002 Forward Poetry Prize (Best Single Poem) for her poem 'She is in the Past, She Has This Grace'.

**Richard Minns** is an independent researcher, currently living and working in Argentina. He is a visiting research fellow at the University of Sheffield, UK.

**Andy Pearmain** is a research student and associate tutor at the University of East Anglia.

**Al-Saddiq Al-Raddi** is one of the leading poets writing in Arabic today. He lives in Omdurman, Khartoum. His books of poetry include *Songs of Solitude* (1996), *The Sultan's Labyrinth* (1996) and *The Far Reaches of the Screen...* (1999).

**Amir Saeed** is a Senior Lecturer in Media and Cultural Studies at the University of Sunderland.

**Richard Wilkinson** is professor of social epidemiology at the University of Nottingham and author of *The Impact of Inequality: how to make sick societies healthier* (Routledge 2005).

**David Wilson** is Professor of Criminology at the University of Central England in Birmingham. He was Senior Policy Advisor to the Prison Reform Trust, and between October 1983 and April 1997 he was a Prison Governor.

EDITORIAL

# Convivial cultures

In this issue we explore questions of how we can live together in a more convivial way. A common theme in many of the articles is the need to address the sense of disconnectedness and alienation that is brought about by living in society where the market invades every part of our lives, including our minds and bodies. Some contributors argue the need for a more humane and democratic politics and culture; others highlight aspects of contemporary life that contribute to inhumanity, or attempt to think through some of the contours of more convivial cultures.

Zygmunt Bauman argues that escape from the pressures of a risk-strewn and deregulated world has become the new meaning of utopia: it now means little more than a constant search to avoid being a loser, the practice of competitive consumption and the remodelling of the self - trying to find the small safe space within the inferno. He evokes a world where there seems little hope of thinking collectively about new ways to live.

In contrast to this world of individuals, Roshi Naidoo discusses the possibility of giving more recognition to our sameness. She argues that we need to think more about sameness, instead of being unremittingly focused on difference. In this she references Paul Gilroy's work on empire and the idea of the possibility of a new version of humanism. As she asks, what would it mean to recognise that the world's poor are just like us, or that Britain is not as special as it thought it was?

Alan Finlayson's contribution to a politics of re-engagement is to think about ways of improving our political rhetoric. He argues the need for a more transformative approach to communication, a move away from holding steadfast to a set of ideas seen as possessions, and towards speaking with, not to, our fellow citizens. A more conversational democracy would clearly be an important part of a more convivial culture.

Pat Kane argues that we would all be a lot less miserable if we thought less about work and more about play. He suggests that work should be renamed valuable activity and play should be understood as creativity, fundamental to the art of life, and a constitutive part of our humanity. This would help us to see where much of the misery of work comes from and to think creatively about ways of making our lives more satisfying. Amir Saeed looks at one specific area of creativity - Islamic hip-hop - and traces fascinating lines of connection between music, identity, creativity and resistance. Jonathan Keane charts the more dysfunctional forms of cultural life but sees hope in the assertion of humanity against the market.

Simon Charlesworth, Paul Gilfillan and Richard Wilkinson discuss the adverse effects of inequality on people's sense of self and health, and this theme of the emotional aspects of living with injustice are taken up in David Wilson's account of the inhumanity of prisons, where he argues that finding ways for people to emotionally engage with prisoners as human beings is the key to campaigning for the abolition of prisons.

Richard Minns tells of the Mothers of May Square, a group who have built a movement full of life from the ashes of the bitter grief of the loss of their children. Richard Gott also brings good news from South America, in his account of the rise of the left there, and in particular the rise of indigenous groups who are now organising to challenge the continuing injustices of their colonial disappropriation.

Elsewhere in the issue, Christoph Bluth gives a very informative account of the geopolitics of Central Asia, Sue Himmelweit outlines the main features of feminist approaches to economics - and Andy Pearmain calls for the Labour Party to be humanely killed off.

SD

**COMMENTARY**

# Wonderful life

## Jonathan Rutherford

> It's a wonderful life if you can find it.
> Nick Cave

In Michael Collins's book *The Keepers of Truth* (Scribner 2001) Bill lives a life of uneventful, quiet desperation alone in a mansion on the edge of a decaying town in the mid West of the US. Close by is the zoo marooned in a post-industrial wasteland populated by the homeless and echoing with the strange noises of the animals in captivity. Bill's grandfather made a fortune manufacturing fridges - 'factories were our cathedrals' - but his family followed the town into penury and despair when production stopped. Bill works as a journalist on the local paper writing mundane stories that keep the gossip mill of small town life turning. But he is bewitched by a desire to speak the truth - the poverty, despair, suicides that plague the town - and truth erupts from him and into print, much to the chagrin of his boss Sam, and the consternation of the local citizens. 'I got this tunnel vision, felt suddenly buried under the debris of our dead industrialism. We were occupying one of the gaps in history that go undocumented, that long silent stupefaction before some other means of survival comes along to save civilization.' Bill must search for the truth outside the rule-bound semiotic system that constitutes the stupefaction. He must find it in the madness of unshared meanings.

Here we are in our own gap in history. Old states of life no longer feel tenable, but what is to come in the future? We live in an afterlife of the post-modern and post-industrial. There is little that is tangible to give us our bearings. Zygmunt Bauman characterises this life as liquid modernity. It is a society of increasingly individualised individuals, which cannot easily hold its shape - it neither fixes nor binds time and space. Fluids flow and yield to the slightest pressure. They drip, flow, gush, swirl, disperse into particles, gather into a flood. When we try and grasp the meaning of society, understanding escapes us like water.[1]

In this liquid modern world our anchor is the culture we can create and which we can share. But the paradox of liquid modernity is that its swirling effervescence suspends us in a state of disoriented inertia. Bauman argues that we are each instructed to create our own biographical exit from this 'socially concocted mess'. But it is an impossible task without recourse to the linguistic tools and cultural artefacts of our interdependency. We need others in order to make narratives which give meaning to our individual selves.

How shall we find the common shared meanings that connect us to others? If they no longer exist how shall we make them? This is not a new predicament. At the beginning of the twentieth century Georg Simmel described modernity as a culture of unrest. Individuals are alienated from one another, not through isolation, but because they have become anonymous in the public realm. Things without monetary value are ignored and marginalised. The meaning of life slips through our fingers. For Max Weber capitalist modernity is 'an iron cage' of 'specialists without spirit, sensualists without heart'. It is a nullity which 'imagines it has attained a level of civilization never before achieved'.

Rainer Marie Rilke struggles with this nullity in his sequence of poems *Duino Elegies* (1923). He searches for words which will express his feeling that something profound in his life is missing. He wants to grasp *life* and to express it in his art. He seeks the solitude that will allow him the inward contemplation of his imagination. But to communicate this inner world requires feeling, and his feelings are dependent upon his relationships with others. His need of others threatens his art, and yet his art means nothing without them. He cannot find the words to describe what it is he does want. He is caught in an ambivalence of need and desire. When Rilke looks at himself it is as an object through the eyes of another. He is a spectator of his life: 'Who, therefore, has turned us around, so that/ no matter what we do, we're in that attitude of someone leaving?'

Rilke's ambivalence resonates with the ambivalences of our own modern consumer society. In three decades the size of our economy has almost doubled. We are richer than ever before and yet economic growth has not provided

---

1. Zygmunt Bauman, *Liquid Modernity*, Polity 2005.

a collective sense of well being. It has brought with it greater opportunities and richness of experience for many, but also increasing levels of inequality, insecurity and unparalleled levels of debt. We are beset by social problems that are individualised and hidden away from public view - mental ill health, loneliness, growing numbers of psychologically damaged children, eating disorders, obesity, alcoholism, drug addiction. Here we are, free consumers, inundated with choice, 'singing in our chains'.

In his book *What Should the Left Propose?* (Verso 2005) Roberto Unger argues that the institutional and discursive structures that we build make us who we are. 'They however are finite, and we are not. There is always more in us, more capability of insight, of production, of emotion, of association, than there is in them'. We are, says Unger, 'context-transcending spirits'. There is something more to each of us that cannot easily be defined in language and representation, and there is also within us something that remains unfinished and open to the world. We can never be reduced entirely to sociological explanation. We know things that we cannot always think. The psychoanalyst Christopher Bollas calls them the 'unthought known'.

Michael Polanyi describes something similar in his idea of tacit knowledge - 'we know more than we can tell'. Government belief in knowledge-driven economic activity has been founded in the idea that tacit knowledge is the intangible of profitability and competitive advantage. Corporate capital has spent several decades finessing knowledge management in an attempt to capture it from its employees. University governance has striven to turn learning and thinking into measurable proxies in order to calculate staff productivity and institutional performance. And, like tacit knowledge, cultural meaning has also been expropriated and utilised for commodity production. Creativity and its raw materials of sounds, words, symbols, images and ideas are disentangled from their social ties in order for them to be commodified and their price calculated. But what capital achieves in its utilisation of knowledge and cultural meaning is the destruction of the very things it covets.

In contrast to this market-based instrumental approach to creativity, Ivan Illich proposes an alternative in the idea of conviviality.[2] People need creative forms of labour and the freedom to make things among which they can live. As

---

2. Ivan Illich, *Tools for Conviviality*, Marion Boyars 2001, p11.

consumers we have access to many services and goods, but we do not have a say in how they are made or the ways in which they are put to use. In other words we are deprived of conviviality. Conviviality is an ethical value, and if it is reduced below a certain level in a society, no amount of industrial productivity and consumption can effectively satisfy the needs it creates. Illich argues that society needs to rediscover our interdependency and with it what he calls 'liberating austerity'. This is not a 'hair shirt' kind of austerity which denies pleasure, but a virtue which excludes only those enjoyments that are destructive of personal relatedness.

Paul Tillich suggests something similar when he describes an 'ethic of joy' that enhances playfulness. He contrasts the idea of joy with the kinds of pleasure we call fun. These, he argues, can be about an escape from emptiness, by which he means a lack of relatedness to things and persons and meanings; even to one's own self. This kind of fun is not the creative kind connected with play. It is ephemeral and distracting, the type of fun which can easily be commercialised, for it is dependent on calculable reactions, without passion, without risk, without love.[3]

There is a certain judgementalism in the moral tone of Tillich and Illich, but they offer suggestive alternatives to the commercially driven fun of consumer culture. We need to create something meaningful that might bridge Bill's gap in history: a transformative politics of the common good, and an imaginative collective projection of ourselves into a hopeful future. We might begin by attending to the madness of unshared meanings - the disorderly profusion of signs that have not been dragooned into the rule-bound semiotic system, as Wendy Wheeler describes it.[4] This is the world of the imagination - unquantifiable and beyond measurement. It has been expunged from official forms of knowledge, and the logic of capital is unable to assimilate it. Imagination emerges out of the unthought known, and offers us the resources of hope.

---

3. Paul Tillich, *The New Being*, Charles Scribner's Sons 1955.
4. Wendy Wheeler, *The Whole Creature: Complexity, Biosemiotics and the Evolution of Culture*, Lawrence & Wishart 2006.

# Living in utopia

## Zygmunt Bauman

*Does the concept of utopia have any meaning in contemporary society?*

The lives of even the happiest of people (or, as the envy-tainted unhappy would have it, the luckiest) are anything but trouble-free. Not everything works in life as one would like. Unpleasant and uncomfortable events abound: things and people keep causing us unexpected and unwelcome worries. And what makes such adversities particularly irksome is that they tend to come unannounced. They hit us, as we say, 'as bolts from the blue'; it is impossible to take precautions and avert these catastrophes, since no one expects a thunderbolt from a cloudless sky. The suddenness of such blows, their irregularity, their nasty propensity to appear from anywhere and at any moment, make us feel defenceless. Danger is free-floating, freakish and frivolous, and we are its sitting targets. We can do little to protect ourselves. Such hopelessness is frightening: uncertainty means fear. No wonder we dream of a world with no accidents. A regular world. A predictable world. Not a poker-faced world. A reliable, trusty world. A secure world.

In the sixteenth century Sir Thomas More gave us the name utopia for such dreams - writing at a time when old and apparently timeless routines were beginning to fall apart, old habits and conventions were starting to show their age, and rituals their seediness; violence was becoming rife (or so it seemed to people unaccustomed to unorthodox turns of events); powers that had hitherto been omnipotent found the newly emerging realities too unruly and unwieldy to be held in check, and too intractable to be tamed in the old and tested ways. Improvisation and experimentation, fraught with risks and errors, were fast becoming the order of the day.

Rightly or wrongly, in the following centuries utopian dreamers had the confidence that it was possible to design a better, fear-free, world, as well as the requisite acumen to lift the 'is' to the level of the 'should-be'. And they had the necessary gumption to carry out the blueprints as well as design them. For the next few centuries, the modern world was to be an optimistic world, a world-living-towards-utopia.

It was also a world in which there was a belief that a society without utopia was not livable, and therefore that a life without utopia was not worth living. If anyone should doubt this, they could always be reminded of its truth on the authority of the brightest minds around. For instance, here is Oscar Wilde:

> A map of the world that does not include Utopia is not worth even glancing at, for it leaves out the one country at which Humanity is always landing. And when Humanity lands there, it looks out, and, seeing a better country, sets sail. Progress is the realisation of Utopias.

With the benefit of hindsight, however, one would be inclined to correct the last sentence: progress tended to be a chase after utopias, rather than the 'realisation' of utopias. Utopias play the role of the rabbit at the dog track - pursued but never caught. Or, even more to the point, progress could be seen as a continuous effort to run away from failed utopias; as a movement away from the 'not-as-good-as-expected', rather than one from 'good' to 'better'. Realities declared to be the 'realisations' of utopias were invariably found to be ugly caricatures of dreams, rather than the things dreamt of. The overwhelming reason to once more 'set sail' tended to be an aversion to what *had been* done, rather than an attraction to what *may be* done yet ...

The views of another wise man, Anatole France, chimed well with those of Oscar Wilde:

> Without the Utopias of other times, men would still live in caves, miserable and naked. It was Utopians who traced the lines of the first city ... Out of generous dreams come beneficial realities. Utopia is the principle of all progress, and the essay into a better future.

For Anatole France, utopias were so firmly settled in the life of day-to-day society that a human existence *without* utopia seemed not only inferior and terminally flawed, but downright unimaginable. It seemed obvious to Anatole France, as it was to many of his contemporaries, that even the troglodytes had to dream their utopias, so that we could live in caves no longer ... How otherwise would we have arrived at Hausmann's Parisian Boulevards? There would be no 'first city' without a 'utopia of city' preceding it. And since we always tend to project our own way of life onto other life-forms that we wish to understand, this view seemed more or less self-evident to successive generations brought up in the pull towards as yet untested utopias, and the push from discredited ones.

And yet, contrary to the view of Anatole France, utopias were born at the same time as modernity, and could only breathe in the modern atmosphere.

## Utopia and modernity

First and foremost, utopia is an image of another universe, different from any universe one knows. In addition, this universe is seen as being entirely originated by human wisdom and devotion - and this idea that human beings can replace the world-that-is with another and different world, entirely of their making, was almost wholly absent from human thought before the advent of modern times. The grindingly monotonous self-reproduction of pre-modern forms of human life left little space for rumination on alternative forms of human life on earth, except in the shape of apocalypses or the last judgment, both of them of divine rather than human provenance.

To be born, the utopian dream needed two conditions. First, the overwhelming (even if diffuse and inarticulate) feeling that the world was not functioning properly and had to be attended to and overhauled to set it right. Second, it was necessary to have confidence in the capacity of humans to rise to the task, the belief that 'we, humans, can do it': that we possess reason, so as to be able to spy out what is wrong with the world and find out what is necessary to replace its diseased parts, and the strength to graft such designs on human reality. In short, that we possess the capacity to force the world into a shape better fit for the satisfaction of human needs, whatever those needs are or may become.

One could say that the pre-modern posture towards the world was akin to that of a gamekeeper, whereas the gardener's attitude serves well as a metaphor for the modern world-view and practice.

The main task of gamekeepers is to defend from human interference the land assigned to their wardenship, in order to defend and preserve its 'natural balance'; the task of gamekeepers is to promptly discover and disable any snares set by poachers, and to stop alien, illegitimate hunters from trespassing. Their activities rest on the belief that things are at their best when not tinkered with; that the world is a divine chain of being in which every creature has its rightful and useful place, even if human mental abilities are too limited to be able to comprehend the wisdom, harmony and orderliness of God's design.

Not so the gardener: they tend to assume that there would be no order in the world at all, were it not for their constant attention and effort. Gardeners know best what kind of plants should and should not grow on the plot entrusted to their care. They first work out the most desirable arrangement in their heads, and then see to it that this image is engraved on the plot. They force their pre-conceived design upon the plot by encouraging the growth of the right type of plants and uprooting and destroying all the others (now re-named 'weeds'), whose unwanted presence disrupts the overall harmony of the design. It is gardeners who tend to be the most ardent producers of utopias.

Today, however, one is always hearing of 'the demise of utopia' or 'the end of utopia', or 'the fading of the utopian imagination'; this has been repeated often enough to have taken root and settled in common sense, and to be taken as self-evident - and this is because the gardener's posture is giving way to that of the *hunter*.

Unlike the gardener or the gamekeeper, the hunter could not care less about the overall 'balance of things' - whether 'natural' or contrived. The sole task hunters pursue is another 'kill', big enough to fill their game-bags to capacity. They would by no means consider it their duty to ensure that the supply of game in the forest is replenished after the hunt. If the woods have been emptied of game, due to a particularly successful hunt, hunters can move to another relatively unspoiled wilderness, still teeming with potential hunting trophies. It might occur to them that sometime in a distant and undefined future the planet could run out of forests. But this is not an immediate worry, and certainly not *their* worry: it won't jeopardise the results of the present hunt, and so it is not a prospect to ponder on - or take action about.

We are all hunters now, are all called upon to act like hunters, on penalty of eviction from the world of hunting - or even relegation to the world of the hunted. No wonder, then, that whenever we look around we are likely to see other lonely hunters like ourselves - or hunters hunting in packs, which we also occasionally try to do. These ways of behaving are known as 'individualisation'. And today we would have to try really hard to spot any gardeners contemplating predesigned harmony from behind their private garden fences and then going out to realise their plans. Nor is it easy to find many gamekeepers whose aim is to protect territories (this being the origin of the anxiety of those with ecological concerns, who try their best to alert the rest of us). That increasingly salient absence is called 'deregulation'.

It stands to reason that in a world populated mostly by hunters there is no room left for utopian musings; and that, were they offered them for consideration, not many people would take utopian blueprints seriously. And even if we knew how to make the world better, and took making it better to heart, the truly puzzling question would then be whether there was anyone with sufficient resources and a strong enough will to do it ... Those and suchlike expectations used to be vested in the resourceful authorities of nation states - but, as Jacques Attali recently observed in *La voie humaine*: 'nations have lost influence over the course of affairs and have abandoned to the forces of globalisation all means of orientation in the world's destination, and any defence against the many varieties of fear'. And the 'forces of globalisation' are not well-known for their 'gamekeeping' or 'gardening' instincts or strategies; instead they favour hunting and hunters. *Roget's Thesaurus*, justly acclaimed for its faithful recording of successive changes in verbal usage, today has every right to list the concept of 'utopian' in close proximity to 'fanciful', 'fantastic', 'fictional', 'chimerical', 'air-built', 'impractical', 'unrealistic', 'unreasonable' or 'irrational'. And so perhaps we are indeed witnessing the end of utopia?

## The utopia of the hunters

I suggest to you that if utopia had a tongue, and in addition was blessed with Mark Twain's wit, it would probably insist that its obituaries have been somewhat exaggerated ... And it would have good reasons to say so. Type 'utopia' on your computer screen, and Google will bring up 4,400,000 websites - an impressive number even by internet standards, and hardly symptomatic of a putrefying corpse, or even a body in convulsions of agony.

Let us, however, have a closer look at the websites listed. The first on the list, and arguably the most impressive, informs us that: 'Utopia is one of the largest free interactive online games in the world - with over 80,000 players'. Then there are some, scattered here and there, with references to the history of utopian ideas and to centres offering courses in that history - catering mostly for lovers of antiques and collectors of curiosities; the most common among them go back to Thomas More himself, the forefather of the whole thing. These websites are a definite minority of entries.

I would not pretend that I browsed through all four million four hundred thousand entries (such an aim in any case could perhaps be seen as being among the most utopian of projects), but the impression I received after reading a statistically decent random sample is that the term 'utopia' has been appropriated mostly by holiday, interior design and cosmetics companies, and fashion houses. All of these offer individual services to individuals seeking individual satisfactions, and individual escapes from individually suffered discomforts.

And another impression I got from my browsing: on the rare occasion when the word 'progress' appears in the homepages of these commercial websites, it no longer refers to a forward drive towards something positive. Far from being seen as a chase after a spinning-along utopia, 'progress' implies a threat, one that makes finding a lucky escape imperative; the term evokes the urge to run away from a disaster that is breathing down your neck ...

Progress, to cut a long story short, has moved from being part of a discourse of shared *improvement*, to become part of a discourse of individual *survival*. Progress is no longer thought about in the context of an urge to rush ahead, but in connection with the need for desperate efforts to stay in the race. We think of 'progress' not when we are working for a rise in status, but when we are worrying about staving off a fall. 'Progress' appears in the context of the need to avoid being excluded from it. You listen attentively to the information that this year Brazil is 'the only winter sun destination', mostly so that you have the necessary knowledge to avoid being seen where people of aspirations similar to yours were being seen *last* winter. Or you read that you must lose the ponchos which were so much in vogue last year: time marches on and wearing a poncho now makes you 'look like a camel'. Or you learn that wearing pinstripe jackets with T-shirts, so much the 'must do' last season, is over - because 'every nobody' does that now ... And so it goes on. Time flows by, and the trick is to keep pace with the waves. If you don't wish to sink, keep surfing - and that means changing your wardrobe, your furnishings, your wallpaper, your look, your habits - in short, yourself - as often as you can manage.

I don't need to add, since it should be obvious, that this emphasis on the disposal of things - abandoning them, getting rid of them - rather than on their appropriation, suits well the logic of a consumer-oriented economy. People sticking to yesterday's clothes, computers, mobiles or cosmetics would spell disaster for an economy whose main concern, and *sine qua non* condition of survival, is the rapid and accelerating assignment of sold and purchased products to waste - and in which swift waste-disposal is the cutting-edge industry.

Increasingly, *escape* is becoming the name of the most popular game in town. Semantically, escape is the very opposite of utopia, but psychologically it is its sole available substitute: one could say that it is its new rendition, refashioned to the measure of our deregulated, individualized society of consumers. You can no longer seriously hope to make *the world* a better place to live in; you can't even make really secure that better *place* in the world that you try to carve out for yourself.

What is then left is the fight against *losing*: try at least to stay among the hunters, since the only alternative is to find yourself among the hunted. And the fight against losing is a task which, to be properly performed, will require your full, undivided attention, twenty-four hours a day and seven days a week; above all it requires that you keep on the move - as fast as you can ...

Joseph Brodsky, the Russian-American philosopher-poet, vividly described the kind of life that has been set in motion by the compulsion to escape. The response of the losers - of the poor - may be violent rebellion or, more commonly, drug addiction: 'In general, a man shooting heroin into his vein does so largely for the same reason you buy a video', Brodsky told the students of Dartmouth College in July 1989. As to the potential haves, which the Dartmouth College students aspired to become:

> you'll be bored with your work, your spouses, your lovers, the view from your window, the furniture or wallpaper in your room, your thoughts, yourselves. Accordingly, you'll try to devise ways of escape ... you may take up changing jobs, residence, company, country, climate, you may take up promiscuity, alcohol, travel, cooking lessons, drugs, psychoanalysis ...

In fact, you may lump all these together, and for a while that may work. Until the day, of course, when you wake up in your bedroom amid a new family and a different wallpaper, in a different state and climate, with a heap of bills from your travel agent and your shrink, yet with the same stale feeling toward the light of day pouring through your window ...

Andrzej Stasiuk, an outstanding Polish novelist and a particularly perceptive analyst of the contemporary human condition, suggests that 'the possibility of becoming someone else' is the present-day substitute for now largely discarded notions of salvation or redemption:

> Applying various techniques, we may change our bodies and re-shape them according to a different pattern ... When browsing through glossy magazines, one gets the impression that they tell mostly one story - about the ways in which one can re-make one's personality, starting from diets, surroundings, homes, and going right up to rebuilding one's psychical structure, often code-named a proposition to 'be yourself'.

Another Polish writer, Sławomir Mrozek, agrees with Stasiuk: 'In old times, when feeling unhappy, we accused God, then the world's manager; we assumed that He did not run the business properly. So we fired Him and appointed ourselves the new directors'. But, as Mrozek, who himself loathes clerics and everything clerical, finds out, business did not improve with the change of management. Once the hope for a better life is focused fully on our own egos and reduced to tinkering with our own bodies or souls, there is no limit to our ambition, and to the temptation to make that ego grow ever bigger, and at the same time to refuse to accept any limits:

> I was told: 'invent yourself, invent your own life and manage it as you wish, in every single moment and from beginning to end'. But am I able to rise to such a task? With no help, trials, fittings, errors and rehashings, and above all without doubts?

The pain caused by unduly limited choices has been replaced by an equal pain, one caused by the obligation to choose while having no trust in the choices made, and no confidence that further choices will bring us any closer to our target. Mrozek compares the world we inhabit to a 'market-stall filled with fancy dresses and surrounded by crowds seeking their "selves"':

> One can change dresses without end, so what a wondrous liberty the seekers enjoy ... Let's go on searching for our real selves, it's smashing fun - on condition that the real self will be never found. Because if it were, the fun would end ...

The dream of making uncertainty less daunting and happiness more permanent by changing one's ego, and of changing one's ego by changing its clothes, is the 'utopia' of hunters - the 'deregulated', 'privatised' and 'individualised' version of old-style visions of a good society, a society hospitable to the humanity of its members. Hunting is a full-time task; it consumes a lot of attention and energy and leaves time for little else. And so it diverts attention from a recognition of the infinity of the task, and postpones *ad calendas graecas* the moment when the impossibility of the task must be faced. As Blaise Pascal prophetically noted centuries ago, what people want is 'being diverted from thinking of what they are ...by some novel and agreeable passion which keeps them busy, like gambling, hunting, some absorbing show ...' People want to escape the need to think of 'our unhappy condition'. And so 'we prefer the hunt to the capture'. The hare itself would not save us from thinking about the formidable but intractable faults in our shared condition, but hunting the hare does the job.

The snag is, though, that once tried, the hunt turns into compulsion, addiction and obsession. Catching a hare is an anticlimax; it only serves to make the prospect of another hunt more seductive, as the hopes that accompanied the hunt are found to be the most delightful experience of the whole affair. Catching the hare presages the end to those hopes - unless another hunt is immediately planned and undertaken.

Is that the end of utopia? In one respect it is - in so far as the early-modern utopias envisaged a point at which time would come to a stop; indeed, the end of time as *history*. There is no such point in a hunter's life, no moment where one could say that the job has been done, the case has been opened and shut, the mission has been accomplished - so that one could look forward to rest and the enjoyment of the booty from now to eternity. In a society of hunters, the prospect of an end to the hunt is not tempting but frightening - since it can arrive only as a personal defeat. The horns will go on announcing the start of another adventure, the call of the hounds will go on resurrecting the sweet memory of past chases, others will go on hunting, there will be no end to universal excitement … It's only me who will be stood aside, excluded and no longer wanted, barred from other people's joys, a passive spectator on the other side of fence, watching the party but unable to join the revellers, at best enjoying the sights and sounds from a distance and by proxy. If a life of continuous hunting is any kind of utopia, it is - contrary to the utopias of the past - a utopia of *no end*. A bizarre utopia indeed, if measured by orthodox standards: the original utopias temptingly promised the end to toil - but the hunters' utopia encapsulates the dream of toil never ending.

Strange, unorthodox utopia it is - but utopia all the same, as it promises the same unattainable prize that all utopias brandished, namely the ultimate solution to human problems past, present and future, and the ultimate cure for the sorrows and pains of the human condition. It is unorthodox mainly in that it has moved the land of solutions and cures from the 'far away' into the 'here and now'. Instead of living *towards* utopia, hunters are offered the possibility of living *inside* utopia.

For the gardeners, utopia was the end of the road; for hunters it is the road itself. Gardeners visualised the end of the road as the vindication and ultimate triumph of utopia. For the hunters, the end of the road would be the lived utopia's final, ignominious *defeat*. Adding insult to injury, it would also be a thoroughly *personal* defeat, and proof of personal failure. Other hunters won't stop hunting, and non-participation in the hunt can only be experienced as the ignominy of personal exclusion, and so (presumably) of personal inadequacy.

Utopia brought from the misty 'far away' into the tangible 'here and now', utopia *lived* rather than being *lived towards*, is immune to tests; for all practical intents and purposes it is immortal. But its immortality has been achieved at the price of the frailty and vulnerability of all who have been enchanted and seduced to live it.

Unlike the utopias of yore, the hunters' utopia does not offer a meaning to life - whether genuine or fraudulent. It only helps to chase the question of life's meaning away from the mind. Having reshaped the course of life into an unending series of self-focused pursuits, each episode lived through as an overture to the next; it offers no occasion for reflection about the direction and the sense of it all. When (if) such an occasion finally comes, at the moment of falling out from the hunting life, it is usually too late for reflection to have any bearing on the way life is shaped - one's own life as well as the life of others - and hence too late to oppose its form or effectively dispute its propriety.

It would be difficult, nay impossible, to sum up the story better than has been already done by the great Italo Calvino, in the words he put into the lips of Marco Polo:

> The inferno of the living is not something that will be: if there is one, it is what is already here, the inferno where we live every day, that we form by being together. There are two ways to escape suffering it. The first is easy for many: accept the inferno and become such a part of it that you no longer see it. The second is risky and demands constant vigilance and apprehension: seek and learn to recognise who and what, in the midst of the inferno, are not inferno, then make them endure, give them space.
> (*La città invisibili*, Arnoldo Mondatori Editore, p164, my translation)

# Fear of difference/ fear of sameness

*The road to conviviality*

Roshi Naidoo

*Does recognising the 'other' as the same as 'us' threaten the fantasy of British uniqueness?*

I recently came across an account of a meeting between Pablo Picasso and Aubrey Williams, the acclaimed abstract painter and key figure in the Caribbean Artists Movement.[1] The two were introduced by Albert Camus, but the meeting was profoundly disappointing for Williams, as Picasso complimented him on his fine African head and suggested Williams should pose for him. This story illustrates two differing but related faces of racism. First, the fetishising of difference as exotic and the only marker of one's humanity, and second - as in Picasso's inability to treat Williams as a fellow artist - the failure to see, for want of a better word, 'sameness'.

In cultural politics it is common to talk about the fear of difference as a crucial component of racism, but this inability to see sameness is not usually described as a fear. However, if we do think of it in this way it may help us to understand what is at stake for those who refuse to see beyond such markers of difference as 'race', sexuality, or disability. What power balances will be disturbed by accepting

---

1. See G. Jordan and C. Weedon, *Cultural Politics - Class, Gender, Race and the Postmodern World*, Blackwell 1995, p446.

both the differences *and* sameness of those around us? And if we understand this, can we see that people hold on to these fears for reasons other than naivety or ignorance? Perhaps there is something more threatening lurking here, which would explain this fear.

This article considers the ways in which fear of sameness, as well as fear of difference, infuses 'race' talk, and the implications this has for British national identity. It looks at how this is played out in various ways in public culture, in representation and in the workplace. But before we can tackle this we need to be clear about what we mean by 'sameness', to avoid it being interpreted as a liberal erasure of difference and a championing of the notion that 'we are all the same under the skin'; such strategies have been used historically to privilege an ethnocentric conformity and to quash and control black political claims.

## Sameness comes with a health warning

Like many people who grew up in the 1960s and 1970s, I was often assured by white school friends and neighbours that I was thought of as being just the same as them, that they didn't notice my blackness and that with them I could be assured that my colour didn't matter. This sort of claim to the acceptance of sameness was obviously problematic: it implied a deracinated view of 'others', a privileging of whiteness as the norm, and an unspoken dislike of those other 'foreigners' who were patently *not* the same and whose differences *did* matter. Even as children we recognised that these sorts of remarks invited us to participate in a very limited idea of our sameness; we knew we were simultaneously like our white friends *and* like those troubling outsiders.

The identity politics of the 1970s and 1980s took issue with this sense of sameness, stressing the power and pleasure of 'blackness' and one's ethnic belonging, socially, culturally and especially politically. Through many of these analyses, being female, black, gay, etc, was recuperated as an important and privileged subject position which conveyed a unique critical vision on the world. Claims that individuals or institutions were 'race blind' were treated with suspicion, and the politics of identity helped us to understand that being told you were the same was in effect being told you were like white people.

Therefore the call for a recognition of sameness, and a stress upon global humanity and our interdependence, brings with it the weight of this history, and the worry that it may involve a loss of a specific black identity, which may in turn undermine the power to speak collectively. Those who have recognised that subjectivity cannot be essentialised and community not homogenised, still feel uneasy when faced with any pleas to an underlying humanity which united us despite our differences.

Another problem with talking about sameness is that it can too easily be harnessed into calls for a normative, dominant Britishness of the prescriptive type implicated in citizenship testing, in the national curriculum, and in tabloid and more 'respectable' views on why we need to exclude migrants and asylum seekers. This version of national belonging can cope with a limited celebration of visible ethnic differences, as long as they are subsumed under a more powerful, universal Britishness. Here you will often find the view that curry is 'our' national dish, an observation usually used to secure a sense of 'new' ease with difference within a largely unaffected national identity. It becomes a signifier of a nation's capacity to be inclusive to its 'legitimate' foreigners, but rarely invites us to reflect on our national myths and conceits.

## Why 'fear'?

Why am I talking about the *fear* of sameness - surely this is just another aspect of our fear of difference? Isn't it just the inability to recognise the humanity of others, and to see that we are essentially similar, that underpins a fear of difference? Although this is true, understanding this as a *fear* allows us to see that there is much for some to be potentially fearful of - such as power shifts, changes in national identity, differing attitudes to migration, a radically different media universe and changes in how we understand the global poor. Whereas there is currently space to acknowledge difference in public culture without undermining the foundations of the state too much, facing the connections between us can potentially expose the deep social, political, cultural and psychological investments there are in how 'race' and difference are currently understood. And possibly the most disruptive idea that lurks within this fear of sameness is that Englishness might not be all that special after all.

Whereas fear of difference is associated with the right, liberals and those on the left define themselves partially through their comfort with difference, and against those who become anxious and fearful in its presence. To be comfortable with difference is often worn of a badge of honour; to shyly insert a reference to how conversant you are with an aspect of 'other' cultures asserts one as cosmopolitan. I don't say this to be dismissive of it, and I don't think it always equates with an exoticisation of cultural difference. But while not to be fearful of difference is one thing - it can mean we are happy to live in multicultural cities or walk down Old Compton Street - can we also accommodate this and still retain a fear of sameness?

## Fear of sameness in national heritage

I recently worked on a cultural diversity project in the heritage sector in a home county. I declined the invitation to work with children of African descent, to talk about African animals at a local natural history museum, and also showed minimal enthusiasm for various multicultural festivals which were suggested. The parts of the project which recorded migration stories, particularly those of Travellers and Gypsies, were more interesting to me, but only, I said, if they were placed in a bigger context of the county's everyday history rather than treated as an exotic add-on to it. Addressing black and 'minority' heritage in Britain, I said, should stop tinkering around the edges and think about the ways in which, for example, the histories of people of Caribbean, African and Asian descent are at the centre of the county's heritage, in the histories of its stately homes, the economies of its industries and in every aspect of its culture.

I made what I thought at the time was a wholly uncontentious claim, that Britain is made up of waves of migration and diaspora and that the legacies of colonialism, domestically and internationally, require closer scrutiny and representation in the heritage sector. However the implication that we are all, in some sense, migrants, and a 'mongrel nation' (as Eddie Izzard's migration history programme was titled) turned out to be a troubling idea. The objections which I met on many (though not all) sides were based on some complex issues which I found could best be theorised around this idea of a fear of sameness.

The rewriting of general narratives of the nation's heritage to locate us as always having been shaped by migration was seen as too diffuse and not as easy as putting on a multicultural event, which could illustrate one's commitment to diversity very clearly. How would people know that it was a diversity project and that the museum sector was now being more inclusive if this approach was taken? It became clear that there was a preference for projects where visible differences could be marked, such as brown faces on websites, different dress, and the evidence of being able to tick the ethnic boxes of audience figures. Without this how would we know we are comfortable with difference?

To be critical of this would seem at first to contradict what I have said about the importance of a radical sameness which incorporates difference. Audience figures for museums and archives show that there is still an under-representation of certain groups and therefore it is only right that special attention is made to bring them in - there needs to be a specific appeal to difference. But we also have to ask whose interests it is in to mark certain differences, and how this works to secure a view of the state as ethnically neutral, magnanimously inclusive and therefore universal. I would be less cynical if this strategy went hand in hand with changing the narratives around the colonial objects in museums, thereby making a more profound commitment to 'ethnic minority' audiences. Asserting sameness denies the state its role as a benign tolerator of 'new' and baffling foreignness - instead it means accepting the fact of us all being caught up in the same historical and geographical momentum.

Accepting this causes fissures in all sorts of national myths, particularly in the casting of the second world war as *the* golden moment of British national identity. When I read Paul Gilroy's *After Empire* I thought immediately of a woman on the project I have been describing who seemed to occupy that place between melancholia for a past England and a pragmatic awareness of the need for a voice for a 'new' multiculturalism.[2] She talked of the first antiracist bus boycotts in England and of the need for more stories to be told in schools about migration to Britain; but this was coupled with an acute sense of loss for 'simpler' times, which was acted out in her participation in second world war and medieval re-enactments. For people who understand British history on this binary of a white past/multicultural present, it is not difference in its present guise which poses a threat, but the fact that it was always so.

In many parts of the local heritage sector the war is by far the most revisited of all historical moments, but sadly not with a view to challenging fascism and anti-Semitism, or as a means of fostering sympathy for those currently dispossessed by war and conflict. Losing oneself in war reminiscences is figured in opposition to the modern and 'politically correct' heritage of cultural diversity. It exists as something safe and knowable, as opposed to something which must reluctantly be embraced. There is space for some acceptance of difference and there is

---

2. Paul Gilroy, *After Empire*, Routledge 2004.

much talk of the 'contribution' of military personnel of Caribbean, African and Asian descent in the war. But the notion of 'contribution' keeps these figures at a distance rather than on the same plane as all those other heroic war figures. What if such soldiers and sailors didn't 'contribute' to the war but won it? Does this interfere too much with our national myths?

'Race' and 'heritage' are concepts which rely heavily on each other to deliver meaning, but have to be kept separate so that the unpleasantness of 'race' doesn't impinge on the purity of 'heritage', and especially on the sanctity of the war as a primary narrative of national greatness. Just as in the adverts currently marketing HP sauce as 'proper British' (though to my knowledge tamarind doesn't grow in abundance in the UK), there is a fantasy of an all-white past of 'proper heritage' which the mongrel nation narrative takes away from us. But to acknowledge our shared mongrel identity would make us think about colonialism, and how British culture was made all over the world. It would also mean recognising that it wasn't just this island of white Britons that held out against the Nazis, but also all the colonial forces.

The mongrel nation narrative also causes ruptures in relation to asylum and migration, particularly in forcing us to acknowledge people's full humanity. For example, even liberal responses to the plight of asylum seekers can often ignore their sameness and only make pleas for the acceptance of their differences. But what if those faceless asylum seekers who feature on the front of the *Daily Express* actually are complex people with the same rights, feelings and desires as 'us'? The dehumanisation of them is so complete that even those whose backgrounds are recently migratory, and who thus could perhaps see similarities more clearly, can be just as vociferous in their dislike of these supposedly disruptive newcomers. A narrative of sameness is very unsettling. For example, what if those graduates working long hours in call centres in India actually have the same aspirations as graduates in Britain, and don't want to spend the rest of their lives in that situation? What if the world's poor are also just like 'us'? If we open up heritage to accepting this migration history, what does it mean in terms of how we should treat today's asylum seekers?

All this means that noting and accommodating difference might not now be the most radical move. It might be that heritage narratives which embrace a radical sameness are more enlightening or challenging than those which only foreground difference. For example, the recent series of the BBC family history programme *Who do you think you are?* located a migrant background, not just for British Asian film director Gurinder Chadha, but also for comedian Julian Clary, and for a figure who is a particular representative of quintessential Britishness, Stephen Fry. To make that migrant connection is in fact a very important step in shifting our understanding of Britishness.

## Fear of sameness in popular culture

Like all those with an interest in the politics of representation, I watch television with a certain degree of anxiety and an annoying tendency to vocalise my interpretation of how 'race', gender, sexuality and other politics are being played out. This has been increasingly focused on whether or not black and 'ethnic minority' characters are allowed to inhabit a space of radical sameness, i.e. one which does not skirt over their differences, yet makes those differences everyday, while also acknowledging their likeness to other characters. It may seem that in most forms of popular culture fear of sameness is not an issue, and one could point to the number of diverse names and faces on news, sport and popular drama. However, we still inhabit a media universe where a panel game of all white men is the norm, and one with all black women would be considered by most to be either a special interest programme or a freak show.

In television comedy this fear of sameness manifests itself constantly. In a comedy landscape full of characters that we laugh at for being disablist, racist, homophobic and sexist, from David Brent to Alan Partridge to Larry David, we know that the presence of an 'other' is there to ensure the joke is delivered and the main protagonist's crassness made clear. Like the heritage sector's need for the ethnic other to announce its inclusiveness, comedies which critique prejudice, no matter how perceptively, rarely include main black characters beyond this function. It is well documented that alternative comedy's commitment to refusing racism, sexism and homophobia as comedy staples did not really translate into the presence of substantially more diverse comedians (Lenny Henry ironically noted how nice it was to see so many of his black brothers and sisters at a recent British comedy awards show). We need to keep asking why this is so.

Generally there is some awareness of racism in its guise as a fear of difference, but do people also understand it as a simultaneous fear of sameness? Sarita Malik in her book on race and representation in British television, explores the ways in which we are offered characters, in soap operas for example, who either exhibit a 'colour blind' sameness or are only marked by stereotypical difference.[3] A constant refrain of television writers over the years has been that they do not know how to write for black characters. But as black actors themselves say, they are not asking people to write great black characters - just great characters that black actors are allowed to play. There is obviously a palpable fear of something going on here - the idea that one would have to write so particularly for a black character seems to suggest that they are baffled by the idea that such a person may have the same hang-ups and preoccupations as everyone else, as well as being baffled by how to deal with their differences. Every decade or so there is great media interest in a role where a black actor is cast as 'everyman', from Sidney Poitier in *Lilies of the Field* (1963), to Denzel Washington in *Philadelphia* (1993), to Will Smith in *Independence Day* (1996). But this would cease being news if there was sustained casting to this end.

There are some exceptions to this is in television comedy, for example Victoria Wood's *Dinner Ladies*. In this ensemble piece set in a workplace canteen, the presence of an Asian woman is banal and commonplace, though she is not deracinated. In a challenge to the 'positive/negative' binary in the politics of representation (if we leave aside the figure of the young black man who fathers her baby), Anita is allowed to be as daft as the others and her difference and sameness are a constant focus of the comedy. In a discussion about faith Anita is asked who they worship in her family. She replies, 'Well we all really like Celine Dion'. There is an episode of the sit-com *Father Ted* which nicely sums up this anxiety about how to address sameness and difference. The hapless priest, in an attempt to prove he is not a racist and make amends to the Irish Chinese community he has offended, holds a multicultural event. The slide show of racial stereotypes ends with a picture of people in China and Ted's proclamation: 'The Chinese - a great bunch of lads'.

A fear of sameness also exhibits itself in the general lack of interest in how black people consume forms of dominant popular culture not deemed to be 'black'. Cultural commentators are straitjacketed into having a view on particular things, and there is a general reluctance to accept that all those big

---

3. S. Malik, *Representing black Britain: a history of black and Asian images on British television*, Sage 2001.

cultural shifts and trends also impacted on black people, whether it is punk rock, Hollywood musicals or decade nostalgia. I am interested in those cultural texts, experiences and identities that are obscured by this refusal to accept that we too lived in Britain through all these things. For example, though much is written about hybridity and expressive cultures around forms such as hip-hop and bhangra, comparatively less has been written about the political expressive possibilities of black consumption of 'white' culture. All this has much to tell us about the complexities of hybrid identities, belonging and national culture. By opening up these avenues and normalising them we can find out more about why it has been so hard for Britons of Asian, African and Caribbean descent to unproblematically belong to Britain.

This is slowly changing. For example, visual artist Mayling To has explored British Chinese identity around *Wham*'s trip to China in the mid-1980s, illustrating how much these neglected areas can tell us about the nuances of identity formation and the politics of belonging. How can we theorise the split between private pleasure and public 'burdens of representation'? What does all this tell us about the ethnicity of the state and its desire to present itself as neutral? How can the private complaints of black artists, academics, curators and others - who are always asked to reflect and comment on black culture, 'race' and racism, but rarely on other things that have shaped them - be articulated in public without it being interpreted as a privileging of 'whiteness'? What did it mean to be an Asian fan of the band the *Smiths* with their fetishising of provisional white Englishness? Is there a fear here that if we too have a view of British culture it dilutes the uniqueness of a white British identity and all the nostalgic preoccupations with spangles, chopper bikes and *Watch with Mother*?

### Fear of sameness in the workplace

I have often thought that the world of academia has many similarities with the world of comedy. Even in humanities departments, where an awareness of the histories of 'race' and the overt and subtle hierarchies it produces are part of everyday life and work, this never quite translates to actually having more diverse staff. Like the comedians who can't move from critiquing racism to actually having all-round black performers in their sit-coms, departments whose bread and butter depends on identifying and rooting out discrimination rarely recruit in ways which reflect this intellectual commitment.

In academia, as in many workplaces, this is not so much to do with a fear of difference. On the contrary, cultural difference is embraced and many black academics will tell you that they have had no shortage of offers to teach anything race-related, irrespective of whether or not it was a specialism. What is said, though, in many sectors including higher education, is that there is a reluctance to recognise expertise beyond 'race' and value the same staff as all-rounders. Every now and then there is an exercise in self-flagellation about this state of affairs, but what is missing is any attendant questioning of why it persists. In whose image are staff being recruited and how is this informed by a culturally specific view of what constitutes a desirable CV? Interestingly, choosing the white candidate miraculously becomes a marker of an ease with difference and an absence of liberal guilt about black people. But it matters that the end outcome is the same as a discriminatory recruitment policy.

## Conclusion

In Gilroy's descriptions of national melancholia punctuated by moments of manic celebration, he identifies many complex, hysterical reactions to being British. In thinking about our similarities to others we raise all sorts of worrying questions about our national worth. What if being British isn't that special after all? What if it is quite banal and we are just like other Europeans? What if we don't have an especially ironic sense of humour? What if we don't necessarily really need an English football coach for the national team as some commentators have recently suggested? Differences of ethnic others can be fitted into current definitions of what makes Britain special, especially in relation to our acclaimed tolerance; but taking us down the road of thinking about the ways in which we are all the same cannot help but cut through the arrogance, presumptions, distortions and half-truths upon which we build our national identity.

The fear of difference is the fear that 'different' people will dilute a stable British identity. However, recognising the 'other' as the same as 'us' disrupts that fantasy of wholeness in a much more profound way. The most threatening 'other' is the one who passes unnoticed amongst us.

# For the sake of argument
## Re-imagining political communication
### Alan Finlayson

*Alan Finlayson argues that the dominant forms of current political discussion are weakening democracy.*

Of the many complaints regularly made about politicians, two are of particular interest and importance: firstly, that politicians don't care what people think; and secondly, that they have no beliefs and simply follow opinion polls and focus groups. These are interesting complaints because individually they seem to be obviously true, common sense in fact. Yet presented together they appear to be contradictory: the first claims that politicians are insufficiently interested in the opinions of citizens, the second that they are *too* interested. This contradiction is not the fault of badly-worded complaints. It exists in the world. Politicians are uninterested in what ordinary citizens think yet simultaneously trapped by their own obsessive need to know exactly that. Meanwhile, many citizens complain about politicians (they lie, they cheat, they are corrupt), yet few will ever discover a politician's views or probity at first hand. The communicative circuits that bind citizens together and that link them with the practitioners of politics are corrupted. Where there should be dynamic and noisy argument, the sound of democratic competition, there is a self-referential silence to which nobody is really listening.

When Aristotle famously defined the human being as the political animal, he did so because of our capacity to communicate with each other, which, he believed, made it possible for us to come to a shared view of what is right and what is wrong, what is good and what is bad. For Aristotle sharing just this mode of communication is the basis of a political community. The priority of communicative over physical conflict has institutional form in our legislature, which is divided into two opposed sides and named as a speaking place, for in it representatives are meant to address each other, making their opinion known while seeking to convince others to share it.

But too often we regard our opinions as precious personal possessions, something to which we have a right, but which it is wrong to impose on others. They are markers of identity (or of what we identify with), and a challenge to them is a threat to the self. Surrounded by advertising, by people eager to part us from our cash, we have an understandable desire to defend ourselves from hidden persuaders and declare argument a bad thing, impolite and inappropriate, and a pseudo-tolerance that allows us to accept another's differences of opinion by never having to listen to them, let alone making clear what we have to say for ourselves.

Democratic politics should be all about the dynamic, creative exchange and transformation of opinions. When opinions become reduced to individual possessions we lose the power of public argument to enhance and change what and how we think and feel. Democracy is correspondingly diminished. Opinions become accessories to which we subscribe (sometimes by direct debit), and trade in them a big business involving magazines, journals, websites, blogs and the industries of opinion-polling and management: politicians partake of such services; democracy apes the marketplace; new kinds of expert try to model political life, predicting its highs and lows the better to manage market share; and the actuaries of government seek the perfect sum that will create the perfect majority, an optimum of satisfaction for all and a permanent majority in Parliament.

But politics is not a game of sums (zero or otherwise). It always takes place under imprecise conditions of uncertainty. Politics is concerned with the future, with the positive or negative consequences of acting or not acting in the present (of going or not going to war, of preparing or not preparing for bird flu, of saving or not saving for pensions), and the future is intrinsically risky and uncertain, requiring us to make judgements of the probable rather than the certain. Even when we do not or cannot possess all the facts, we may still have no choice but to act. These two kinds of uncertainty are common to many kinds of decision, but in public political life an additional and rather special source of uncertainty lies in the fact that people possess very different world-views. They understand and express their interests in various ways and may even understand any particular matter in radically different terms. The place where these heterogeneous world-views and multifarious forms of expression meet is the place of politics, where collective decisions must be taken even when there is no clear ground on which to base them. Here political actors present their interpretations of the situation, visions of the world and proposals for what we should do; they must find the arguments around which different peoples can form a common view and act in concert.

This is the work of rhetoric, the art of persuasion, the presentation of reasons to think (or not think) a particular thing. Unlike philosophical argument, in seeking to motivate us to a common course of action, rhetoric openly employs emotional, ethical and artistic as well as rational appeals. This may assist demagogues urging war on some demonic other, but it can also help those who want us to fight poverty or defend our environment from despoliation. Because they take place under conditions of uncertainty and contestation, public political arguments require more than the logical demonstrations of the seminar room, textbook or think-tank. In situations the very meaning of which is disputed we come to agreement and are motivated to act by the artful presentation of reasons of all kinds. Such moments of persuasion join the political actor and the citizens, binding them in a mutual understanding, a sharing of ideas (albeit ones that are most likely temporary). The first rule of rhetoric (as found in the ancient manuals or the contemporary textbooks) is that a speaker must adapt to their audience, providing reasons that justify a claim in ways the audience may engage with. This is neither craven nor deceitful but an acknowledgement that persuasion is always inter-subjective, an attempt to open the way to some kind of common ground, taking us to a new place where, in forging a meeting of minds, we find we all are changed.

But this kind of transformative communication is rare and the contemporary ecology of communication is not likely to support it. The news and culture industries are the unchallengeable rulers of the public sphere. They possess a power which, unlike that of the military, the judiciary and the government, has no clear place in our constitution and thus exists without safeguards, checks or balances.

Journalists think it their role (rather than that of citizens) to hold politicians to account, and are so much a part of the machinery of power that they want little more than a secure place at the court of Westminster. Media in a capitalist system, necessarily concerned to make a profit, instrumentalise the world. Newspapers or broadcast current affairs programmes compete with each other for viewers, prestige and importance, which means that their interest only incidentally lies in actual politics and primarily with 'the story' - a sellable narrative of relatively uniform type, which, as Sarah Benton has pointed out in this journal, is usually centred on exposures, secrets and intrigue conforming to a readily recognisable archetype: the leader beset by dark forces or hampered by buffoons; secret conspiracies; the soporific people awaiting the new young fresh face that will awaken them to glory once again (see 'Political News', *Soundings* 5).

In addition to these problems arising from the extrinsic features of current affairs media, the intrinsic nature and generic format of news almost always inhibits democratic participation. Newspaper and broadcast news media are fundamentally monological, ill-suited to the encouragement of open-ended and involved argument. The strange anonymity of broadcast media, the impersonal nature of speaking to nobody while speaking to everybody, disrupts rhetorical encounters, since it is not clear who the broadcaster is speaking to, and modification for each audience becomes difficult to achieve. And the manner towards political figures adopted by celebrity interviewers keen to maintain their macho image closes down argument almost completely. This may seem counter-intuitive, since such celebrities like to present what they do as robust and precisely argumentative rather than deferent. But news anchors are not required to advance any argument of their own. Because they are supposed to uphold the pretence of neutrality these interviewers ask only prosecutorial questions, demanding that political actors confirm or deny that this or that took place, was said or was written, seeking to elicit promises or guarantees that can be held against the politician in further encounters.[1] When it does stage an argument broadcast news media always defines the possible conclusions in advance, a yes or no, right or wrong.

---

1. I have developed this point further in 'The Problem of the Political Interview', *Political Quarterly*, Vol. 72, No. 3, 2001. A text of immense value in understanding the effect of broadcasters' 'neutrality' is still Stuart Hall, Ian Connell and Lidia Curti's *The 'Unity' of Current Affairs Television*, published as CCCS Working Papers in Cultural Studies, No.9, 1977.

The terms of decision making are not up for debate (and there are always only two sides). This legalistic mode of inquiry belongs to the rhetorical genre of forensics. It is appropriate for the establishment of what has happened in the past, but not much use for the political arena, where it is the uncertain future and our collective movement towards it that concerns us. The reduction of issues to an inviolable either/or secures the citizens in their place as spectators, audience members allowed only to present a thumbs-up or thumbs-down.[2]

But for all the costs the media impose on them, politicians find it much easier to manage a small group of journalists (whom they know well and were probably at university with) than to deal with an unpredictable public that frames issues in unexpected ways. Indeed, the party politician and the professional journalist very effectively exclude the public, while the interchange of the two is now so common it is barely remarked on. As Neil Postman remarked in the 1980s: 'Political figures may show up anywhere, at any time, doing anything, without being thought odd, presumptuous, or in any way out of place ... they have become assimilated into general television culture as celebrities'.[3] From book-launch to game-show appearance to television presenter is today a not uncommon career path for politicians (and sometimes for their advisers and civil servants). Enamoured of the media they hope might make them famous, many political figures rarely use it to advance any sort of worthwhile argument. In any case politicians and their advisers are generally very bad rhetoricians and would not know a decent argument if it stood up in the House of Commons and called for

---

2. The poet George Szirtes remarks (in an entry on his web diary dated 17.12.05): 'As usual I wake early before the Today programme starts. The focus was, naturally enough, the agreement or otherwise on the EU budget. Humphrys finished by pressing Blair on whether it was success or failure. *Come on, which was it.* And that is where we are. Either something is a success or a failure, good or evil, innocent or guilty, first or nowhere, cheer or boo. It is a perfectly idiotic position for anyone of intelligence to take. I don't know whether it is characteristically English - I doubt it - but it is common. As the poet (me, in this case) says:
   Welcome to England, the land of the Pound.
   Where judges are wigged and monarchs are crowned,
   Where, whether you're Jack Flash or Roger the Dodger,
   The war cry is bound to be *Wanker!* or *Gotcha!!*
3. Neil Postman, *Amusing Ourselves to Death*, Methuen 1987, p135. For a broader analysis of the interplay of politics and celebrity see John Street, 'Celebrity Politicians: Popular Culture and Political Representation', *British Journal of Politics and International Relations*, Vol. 6; and for a number of considerations of the broad politics of 'celebrity' see *Mediactive 2, Celebrity*, edited by Jo Littler.

their resignation. This failing is not simply personal. It is institutional and cultural. The modern speech-writer is not charged with persuading anybody of anything but with ensuring that the right soundbite appears on the news (which will report ten seconds of the speech to support two minutes of the reporter's interpretation); with incorporating the requisite moments to appease or entice various factions and electoral sub-groups; with producing something to please everyone (or at least not offend them) rather than something that might cause people to come away with a perspective different to that with which they started.

A fundamental feature of the formal political process in the twentieth century has been its transformation from a vocation into a professional career from which one expects to make a living for a lifetime, and for which one requires certain technocratic skills. As the amount, range and scale of the things that states are expected to deliver has increased (health-care, education, a stable economy, etc), and as politicians have come to be held directly accountable for them, they have increasingly become bureaucratic functionaries. The bureaucratic mind does not care for arguments other than those contained within the pre-set rules of procedure. For the bureaucrat what is right is what works; the question of what it is we *should* be doing - the political and ethical question - is irrelevant and a distraction from carrying out the allotted task. The political work of persuasion has been farmed out to the professional political marketer, whose task is not to change opinions but to manage them, treating citizens as a collection of pre-set preferences to be juggled or, in a phrase of Stuart Hall's, 'focus-grouped into place'. The more such techniques are deployed, the less loyalty to the political process citizens hold beyond its capacity to satisfy their current preferences. This weakens the ability of anyone to co-ordinate collective activity at the very moment when, if we are to address problems of pensions, healthcare, education, respect or prejudice, we need a concerted collective effort to change our own and each other's thinking and behaviour. Cut off from citizens, political leaders become ever-more dependent on market research; their attempts at collective co-ordination fail to involve or even to be properly addressed to the very people who will carry them out; their words come to seem like vacuous and self-regarding moralism, and the more of it we hear, the more we become both bored and suspicious. The chances of anyone believing what a politician thinks needs to be done sink ever lower, and the demand for better focus groups and marketing ploys to maintain support or consent becomes yet more intense.

This is the cycle of political disaffection. Reduced to the manipulation of fixed preferences and interests, eschewing the process of arguing and changing views, the political process has become separated from everyone who is not a political professional. Debate is narrowed down to focus on technical and technocratic matters rather than the things that underlie them, the principles that might animate us, our sense of what we think we are and what we think we want to do, the utopian horizon to which we might want to lead each other.

Underneath these problems with media coverage of politics and the activities of politicians there is a deeper problem: the places where engaged and transformative political argument might take place are few and definitely far between. Over the last twenty to thirty years British society has done a good job of demolishing or abolishing all the institutions and locations that might host or make possible such debate (and there were not very many in the first place): churches, unions, political parties, voluntary associations. Such sites could not only host discussions and exchanges of opinion, but could feed it through into wider realms and even into the political process. Societies cannot help but establish mechanisms for such exchange (they would not be societies without them), and as these venues have been emptied we have recreated them in various virtual forms: daytime talk shows (sometimes full of passionate debate about the way world is and might be); the seemingly endless run of reality game shows that announce what we do and do not collectively approve of (transsexuals overcoming adversity, faded celebrities who keep the show going without too much whinging).

Such instances of heavily-managed but almost-social discussion belong to the category of rhetoric called 'epideictic', the exhortation to praise or denigrate something. This is currently the dominant mode of public discourse. The tabloid newspapers (and today almost every newspaper is a tabloid) parade before us various celebrities, politicians (and regular people unfortunate enough to get trapped in some media spectacle), seeking to persuade us to take up the role of pantomime audience and boo or cheer as appropriate. This celebration or denigration, a process of sorting out our collective good and bad eggs, reinforces certain conceptions of the socially acceptable and with it some form of public identity. Epideictic is intrinsically conservative (though not in an ideological sense), for it is concerned with the way things are: with an *affirmation* of a given identity rather than with what we might become.

But there is no single dominant identity in our culture. The way communication is disseminated and consumed is undergoing a major transformation (thanks to cable channels, tv-on-demand, internet downloading) and this development in mass broadcasting makes it easy for us to carve out our own small worlds of news and political or social discussion and to live entirely within them. Each of these worlds is filled with the kind of rhetoric that reinforces an identity by means of praise and blame. This is certainly the case across those Conservative media outlets in the US that regard all liberals as porn-toting, drug-using abortionists eager to steal your money in taxes and hand it over to perverts. But it is also true of much of what passes for liberal or left-wing communication, which is always ready to assert a simple oppositional stance in order to reaffirm the virtue of its adherents. To take just one example: Michael Moore's well-known documentary *Fahrenheit 9/11* advances an epideictic rather than political-deliberative argument. Its message is that Bush is bad and it exhorts us to boo him while failing to advance any positive case. For this reason the film may seem like good propaganda but it is essentially self-regarding, affirmative of the views of those who already agree with it and unlikely to change the mind of anybody else. Unfortunately this is the case with many of the current spate of 'political' documentaries and with much political satire. They reinforce rather than subvert or extend political identities. Radical political argument joins with the more obviously reactionary forms of communication in reinforcing positions and spreading the general view that the political process itself is entirely corrupt and worthy not of engagement but of mockery and rejection.

## Connecting differently

This is a gloomy picture verging on the negatively epideictic. Could we do things differently? Politicians could take the time to develop their ways of thinking and speaking beyond that taught to them in media training, finding ways to make their case directly, to advance arguments rooted in general claims about their values and how the world might be. They could spend the time to find out about the worlds in which citizens live and find ways to connect to them. Political media and current affairs programming do not have to maintain their current form. They do not have to employ a tedious array of professional opinion-mongers. It is surely possible to imagine mediated political discussion that is neither didactic nor needlessly populist, that breaks with monological and heavily managed modes of communication and that seeks to encourage the arts of rhetoric that present us with ways to re-imagine the world we have made, the better to act upon it. We could certainly talk about the doings of politicians in Westminster much less (they rarely have anything novel to contribute), be a little less proud of ourselves for poking fun at them (as if this was big, clever and not a way of reinforcing their status), and instead seek the views of those outside the formal political process beyond the limited format of question and answer.

But professional politicians and news journalists are unlikely to change anything spontaneously. So what of those political actors outside the official worlds of media and Westminster politics? Many political activists appear rather uncertain about who or what they are speaking to. Who, for instance, were the clowns who demonstrated at the G8 summit in Scotland addressing?[4] They certainly had no intention of trying to present persuasive arguments to the leaders of the world's capitalist democracies. But they surely did not expect their neo-situationism (with a dash of Bakhtin) to be taken up by the average citizen (although they may well have intended to make quite good television and BBC4 duly made a documentary). Such actions, engineered confrontations with representatives of presumed authority, reinforce the myth that sovereignty and power are located in one place and are the possession of the politician, while affirming the virtuous identity of the one who protests against it. This is yet more self-regarding epideictic: an opportunity to boo in the presence of each other without touching a single fellow citizen. There is a tendency on the left, infrequently acknowledged by us, to dwell within self-regarding arrogance. It is part of our radical puritan heritage, enhanced by the vulgar Marxist myth that the forces of history are on our side, and the anarchist illusion that we possess the untainted virtue of the pure outsider. Such self-assurance seeks reassurance and finds it in the very same fantasy of evil leaders and duped innocents that we criticise so well when we find it expressed by the right.

If we want to change the world we must believe in democracy and in the transformative power of argumentation. We must take our argument to the places that count. And this is not the G8 summit. Democratic politics takes

---

4. I mean the Clandestine Insurgent Rebel Clown Army who explain themselves at www.clownarmy.org/.

place when we stop looking up at the evil powers we despise and down at the toiling masses only we can liberate. It starts when we look from side to side at each other, at our fellow citizens with whom we share this society. Egalitarianism resides in the act of seeking to persuade another, acknowledging that the other can understand what I understand but needs to be convinced for themselves, not taken for granted or told what to do.

The voters of America's 'red states', surrounded by run-down agricultural businesses and mall-stripped towns, should not be voting for the people who put them in that situation. US linguist and rhetorician George Lakoff has demonstrated very clearly how the American right systematically invested in a communicative and intellectual infrastructure to help it successfully 'frame' issues in ways that would favour conservative causes, connecting conservative policy and values with the routine perspectives and values of particular American communities.[5] Progressives cannot win such people over by ignoring them and certainly not by making fun of them as ignorant hicks (which is very often what we do).

In the UK, the left and other progressives have to realise that the way to make headway on issues such as equality, environmentalism or asylum is to win people over by winning the argument. And the people who must be won over are those who have not yet heard about our cause: our neighbours, our colleagues, people we just happen to meet. We must take our arguments out of our own little worlds and into the world at large, to those around us as well as to the TV talk-shows and the radio phone-ins. To succeed at this we must also understand where other people come from, the worlds they live in, and the beliefs they cling to. That requires of us a willingness to adapt to those views, the better to articulate them with our own, and the precondition for this is the willingness to be challenged ourselves; to have our own self-assurance and self-identity exposed. We must discover our rhetorical abilities and cultivate a political spirit that eschews the spectacular but self-regarding action for the act of communication with those who have yet to be convinced, the patient work of speaking not only to others but with them. That, for the sake of argument, is democracy.

---

5. See George Lakoff, *Moral Politics: How Liberals and Conservatives Think*, University of Chicago Press 2002; and (with Howard Dean and Don Hazen), *Don't Think of an Elephant: Know Your Values and Frame the Debate: The Essential Guide for Progressives*, Chelsea Green Publishing Company 2004. See also his Rockridge Institute programme for 'strategic reframing': www.rockridgeinstitute.org/projects/strategic/framing.

# The power of play

## Pat Kane

*Pat Kane argues that workers in post-industrial societies are moving away from the work ethic, towards more playful, but also potentially more caring, forms of activity.*

We - and by 'we' I mean the richer nations of the world - are in a state of crisis about work: about what we do when we work, what it does to us when we work, even what the very nature of work is. There are some major themes on the crisis of work that have become clear over the last five years:

♦ *Work isn't making us happy* - Richard Layard's book *Happiness*, published in the UK (Penguin 2005), and Clive Hamilton's *Affluenza*, published in Australia (Allen and Unwin 2006), both highlight how the prodigious post-war ascent in levels of GDP in the countries of the richer parts of the world has been accompanied by a steady flatlining of reported levels of happiness (with Japan and Sweden as interesting anomalies to this). Beyond a certain level of income, relative to spending power, we don't get that much happier the richer we get. We may well have become more productive (both by using new technology *and* increasing our working hours). But the extra fruits of our labours - the consumerist model of house, car, holidays, malls, treats and toys (adult as well as childish) - do not seem to bring us greater happiness and meaning. If so, what's the point?

♦ *Work is making us unhealthy* - There's a huge amount of recent research on this. Michael Marmot's Whitehall Study on the British Civil Service, with a data-set of over 10,000 subjects, tracked over forty years to the present day, reveals that those civil servants with more choice, autonomy, resources and decision-making power in their jobs live considerably longer than those with less decision-making power. This latter group are much more prone to the onset of ill-health. (Marmot assesses that only a third of this differential is due to more self-abusive lifestyles in the lower ranks - smoking, drinking, etc.) This, to me, is a more devastating point than the usual, and correct, complaint about the overall-rise in working hours, and the consequent stresses, indebtedness and strained family relations. The inequalities of power and status that most of us might accept as the somewhat tedious price of working for a stable organisation are, literally, toxic and death-dealing.

♦ *Work is making us confused* - There is a crisis of identity. What does it mean to be a good or respected worker these days? This is a crisis of what we've come to know as 'the work ethic'. Again, a huge body of research details a broadening and deepening disaffection with this legacy of Puritanism and the industrial revolution. There is a widespread reaction against the attitude that work diligently performed, no matter the extent to which it expresses the talents or sensibility of the worker, is the minimum badge of social respectability.

♦ As Richard Sennett notes in *The Culture of the New Capitalism* (Yale 2006), diligence and commitment to a particular task or craft - one dignity that adherence to the work ethic afforded - is no longer respected, in the flexible and endlessly adaptive modern company. Yet the sheer acrobatics involved in that 'new work' - where individual self-reliance (on a short-term contract) is invoked in the service of an often asphyxiating corporate 'vision' - is hardly a more attractive alternative. The rise of 'stress' as a factor in our working lives is due to this lurch from a 'work ethic' to an 'enterprise ethic'. Madeleine Bunting, writing in *The Guardian* back in January 2003, notes that, in the UK, the number of days lost to individual 'sickies' in the late 1990s and early 2000s, is actually greater than the total number of days lost to collective strikes in the dreaded early 1970s. The crisis of the work ethic is easily summed up in one sentence. Why believe in work, when it doesn't really believe in you?

All these elements add up to a general crisis of meaning and purpose, for countries whose leaders and establishments believe that the most stable social identity available comes through work. Let's try to imagine an answer to these crises. The first thing I want to do is to rub out the word 'work', and replace it with a clunkier term like 'valuable activity'. What is the 'valuable activity' that could make us happier, make us healthier and make us clearer in our minds (rather than confused) about who we are, and what we want?

## The power of play

The first thing to say about play is that it's not what you think it is. Or, to be exact, it's much *more* than you think it is. For most of us, at the level of daily speech, play is what children do, or what adults do sometimes in sport, or at parties. For some of us, play connotes the idea of creativity (as in theatre and music), or enterprise and strategy (as in politics and business). For a certain younger generation - and increasingly beyond them - play is what they largely do with their interactive technologies and communication devices.

Play is actually an extremely pervasive and elemental term in our language. We easily move from what we think is its most obvious definition (the mere activity of children) to something which is, to use an extremely Scottish word, epistemological - that is, play as a way of framing what counts as true in our material and social world. And beyond that, our meanings become even cosmic or spiritual. Most creation myths are acts of play - the sheer gratuity of 'Let there be light' in genesis; the dice tumbling from the hands of Mahabarata; the permanent play of forms and connections in Hinduism and Buddhism.

The reason why play travels so promiscuously across our worlds of meaning goes all the way back to the child at play. For without play, we simply would not develop as advanced mammals. In a very direct and causal way, play enables the entire human condition. The psychologist Brian Sutton-Smith, in *The Ambiguity of Play* (Harvard, 1997), says that for humans (and mammals), play is 'adaptive potentiation'. It describes the kind of things we see our children do in their play spaces and play times. The density of our infant brains, the weakness of our infant bodies, and the complexity of our relationships with other young humans, means that we need a zone in our early years in which we can literally test out all this sophisticated biological and psychological equipment.

The need to play is so strong that the more complex adult mammals ensure that there are play times, play spaces and play resources - a patch of protected ground, supplies of food, maybe even materials - to enable this development through play to happen. And the end point of human play, its outcome, has been our species dominance on this planet, through our sheer capability and flexibility as organisms. If play is so constitutive of our humanity, the psychological and biological starting-point of all our complexities and capacities, why do we think that at a certain stage in our development, we must stop playing, 'put childish things behind us', become non-playful, perhaps working adults? I think the elemental key to this lies in the relationship between play and scarcity, or (the same thing) play and abundance.

The young mammal at play needs the labouring adult mammal to provide the resources for play, whether that's defence of territory or basic sustenance. That is, developmental play occurs best in an environment which *is some distance from immediate survival* - even if the skills learned in play (hunting, status management, various ingenuities of perception) are skills that will help the mammal contribute to basic survival, her own and her progeny, when she is older. The further we move from scarcity as human animals, through our capacity to 'do more with less' through the application of science and technology, the more opportunity we have to extend the moment of play throughout our adult lives.

## Play isn't leisure

In my understanding of the word, play is not leisure - if we understand 'leisure' to be that compensatory activity we conduct after our 'necessary labours' have been completed, a 're-creation' of our exploited selves in order to return to our duties. If play is 'adaptive potentiation' - that is, the spinning-out of possibilities, experiments and imaginings to ensure our continuing development and adaptability - then our play is as 'necessary' to our survival (and thrival) as our work. The problem with the leisure society vision is that it usually presumed a kind of well-managed, semi-bureaucratic, 'steady' state, with productive automation of various kinds purring away in the background, and usually an alarmingly homogenous population living in quiet consensus.

Yet, as we know, our societies have become far more conflictual, disruptive, emergent and surprising than the leisure theorists could ever have imagined. In the face of the challenges presented by feminism, environmentalism, fundamentalism, monetarism, globalism and informationalism, the last thing our response could ever be is 'leisurely'. We need to be players in this accelerating world, not idlers or strollers or contemplatives.

## 'Why are they so unhappy?'

I occasionally consult to large organisations in the private and public sectors. And I often have some sympathy for the senior managers and executives I talk to, as they try to respond to the levels of unhappiness, discontent and lack of motivation that they face in their workforces, who are often operating under conditions which - seen from the perspective of the leisure society theorists of the 1970s - might seem like a partly-achieved utopia. And, seen from the perspective of working conditions in the first half of the twentieth century, they might seem like a real one. 'What can we do to address these issues?' I am asked. 'What else can we do?' My response is rarely satisfying to them - which is why I'm only an occasional consultant. (Or a deconsultant, as I often call myself - someone who goes into an organisation, unravels everything into a fertile mess, and is rarely invited back.)

What I usually say is that they are facing a workforce whose very twenty-first century skills - the ability to communicate well and respond empathetically, to respond nimbly and enterprisingly to new tasks, to use networks with ease to collaborate with others and inform themselves - are not skills that can be ultimately be harnessed to the ends or goals of any organisation. These are the skills of the *ars de vivre*, of the arts of life themselves.

This is a workforce which is not just better educated, healthier and longer-lived, but which also has access to an ethical perspective on their organisations - the product of feminism, environmentalism and increasingly spirituality - which they find difficult to bracket off from their day-to-day activities and work duties. Their discontent is a discontent of sheer potential: what do I do with my life, my capacities? What is my purpose? Is this the right place, with the right structure and the right people, to manifest that? Material abundance has generated ethical anxiety, not complacency.

Again, after all that, the executive will come back to me again: 'so what *can* I do then?' My response is to suggest that they recognise that this restlessness comes from a very deep place - the place of play, that wiring which compels to explore, self-develop and potentiate, whenever we feel we have sufficient distance from necessity (and, for most of us in the richest parts of the world, that is a steadily increasing distance).

So, I propose, could they consider turning part of their workspaces into playgrounds? By which I don't mean a 'leisure' or 'recreation' space, the pool table or Playstation machine in the games room. But actually offering up the resources, both human and technical, of the organisation to support the diversive explorations, the adaptive potentiations, the developmental play, of their staff - whether relevant to the company's overall directives or not.

It's at this point the conversation usually peters out, with everyone rushing from my playshop to get back to their groaning in-boxes and time-shifted meetings. In my experience, it's a rare organisation which can face down their accountants and shareholders, or (if in the public sector) their political masters, and genuinely respond to the crisis of working values - or, looked at from my perspective, the renaissance of play values - that's happening within their workforce. It seems to be a limit within conventional forms of organisation, that they can rarely imagine that they exist in a condition of abundance - whether of material or human resources.

At one level - the micro, bottom-up level - there is much evidence of a broad culture of substantive play, manifesting itself through our active use of interactive technology, our diverse pop cultures, and our 'lifestyle militancy' about nurturance and self-development. Yet there is another level - the macro, top-down level - which is also promising. At least in some of the richer parts of the world, particularly Europe, some legislators and statespeople are becoming aware that the 'grounds of play' can only be secured by regulation and policy. The state becomes an active supporter - and more importantly, a legitimator - of a variety of forms of valuable human activity, not just those which can be commodified. The state thus ensures that the full range of adaptive potentiations that humans might pursue, *are* pursued - and not just those edited and selected by a marketplace.

Examples of this might be the tenaciously maintained 35-hour week in France, which has resulted notoriously in both an increase in leisure and self-improvement activities (without reduction of overall economic productivity), and in a baby boom (a non-marketplace activity which speaks for itself). Holland's policies on social 'flexicurity' - where part-time work is given exactly the same status in protection, rights and hourly rates as full-time work - allows for a rich mix of activities (both economic and social, familial and recreational).

Scandinavian examples of strong state support of citizens' autonomy - from Finland's free high quality education system, from primary to university, to the income supplements and sabbatical allowances built into labour law in Sweden, Denmark and Norway - are legion. Yet none of these schemes are themselves sufficient to address the aspirations of a players' identity: more radical, less conditional schemes - such as the variety of basic income or basic capital options, as suggested by writers like Claus Offe or Bruce Ackerman - might be more appropriate (though as yet untried in practice). If these pressures at the micro and the macro level can intensify, it is possible that daily life in our institutions and enterprises will more lastingly change.

But what I want to stress very strongly is that these organisational changes *are impeded by the very vocabulary of work itself*. The cultural and historical weight of work - particularly the legacy of Puritanism - means that it is a poor and crude description of the subtle range of creative actions that we actually pursue, and would want to pursue more intensely, in our information-age organisations. And the ethical residue of work - that sense of duty to others, the notion of 'good works' - I think should be properly called 'care', rather than bound up in a term which can make our altruism and empathy seem like a functional necessity. So between 'play' and 'care', in my view, we can get rid of the term 'work' altogether. And with that mind-forg'd manacle loosened, we can begin to devise institutions and organisations that respond to our growing sense of genuine playfulness.

### How many ways to play?

Sutton-Smith has outlined what he regards as the seven major 'rhetorics' of play - the main ways in which play has been valued in human culture. He divides them into the modern and ancient rhetorics of play:

### Modern

*Play as progress* - we adapt and develop through play
*Play as selfhood* - play as an expression of voluntary freedom
*Play as imaginary* - play as symbolic transformation, mental energy

### Ancient

*Play as power* - we contest and compete with others - in sports and games, in theatres of power

*Play as identity* - the play-forms we use to confirm membership in a community - carnival, ritual, festival
*Play as fate and chaos* - the sense that we are played by forces greater than ourselves, not accessible to reason
*Play as frivolity* - play as laughter, subversion, tomfoolery

A significant amount of human social order is expressed through these rhetorics of play. The ancient play-themes are as alive in our existences as the modern ones. If there is a more philosophical definition of play that unites these rhetorics, it comes from Friedrich von Schiller, author of the first great play theory, *Letters on the Aesthetic Education of Man* (1794). Schiller said that play means to 'take reality lightly'. The etymological root of play is even more appropriate, from the Indo-European *-dlegh*, meaning 'to engage, to exercise yourself'.

Certainly, those first five rhetorics - play as self-development, play as voluntary will, play as imagination, play as power, play as identity - seem like the skill-set of the very best enterprises we could conceive. And what is powerful about the remaining two rhetorics - play as fate, play as frivolity - is that they are an in-built caution to the over-confidence or presumptiveness of the preceding five.

I have attempted a 'play audit' of organisations, using these seven rhetorics, among non-executive-level workforces. But often the very constrictions of these organisations, whether it's their hierarchy or corporate identity or strategic goals, means that (at the end of my audit) workers can become incredibly dissatisfied with their existing conditions. (Again, fulfilling my role as a deconsultant ...) The audit either shows up how much they are maxing out on certain kinds of play (often identity and power, in terms of a competitive corporate identity); how they are impoverished in some forms (say, play as freedom and as imagination, in terms of the unengaging and uninspiring nature of their tasks); and are positively toxic in others (play as frivolity, translating as the darkest office humour and parody).

But I still think the rhetorics - or some other typology of playful activities conducted beyond scarcity - would be a useful tool for any start-up organisation, whether a commercial or social enterprise, particularly one that accepted the player-nature of their employees/stakeholders, and that wanted to ensure every possibility for 'adaptive potentiation' was being nurtured throughout the design of their company, and its product or service. I live in hope.

## The techno-politics of play

Information and communications technology (ICT), as it is applied and used within traditionally-structured organisations, doesn't just replace routine human mental labour; it also over-works and over-controls those humans who remain. But thankfully, ICT does not begin and end in the organisation. Indeed, in terms of participation, local custom, and the transmission of traditions and forms, cyberculture is one of the most powerful and authentic 'folk' cultures ever created.

The World Wide Web was originally conceived as a 'play' technology by Tim-Berners Lee - a way for scientists to play brain tennis with each other's papers and documents, across long distances. Much of the essential architecture of the internet has been created by enthusiastic programmer amateurs, who then gifted their creations to the electronic commonwealth. The most notable, and explicitly playful, of these was Linus Torvalds, who created the operating system Linux in the early 1990s as a post-grad student, which has now grown into a low-or-no-cost alternative to Microsoft, embraced by giants like China and Brazil.

Cyberculture is deeply congruent with the notion of play as a possibility generator, helping us to survive and thrive by generating potential options. Net culture is, I would assert, one of the first authentic institutional responses to our emerging play-identity. Its implicit ethos is the creation of robust, repairable, reliable collective infrastructures, which nevertheless allow and encourage a multitude of enterprises and initiatives from the individuals and groups that use them. It is almost directly analogous with that mammalian play moment I discussed earlier.

The internet is just like that defensible, well-resourced space for young complex mammals, protected by responsible guardians (which, at least up until this point, the elders of cyberspace - the hacker priesthood - have largely been), within which much developmental frolicking, testing and experimenting can take place. Now we *could* argue about how much playful development is actually occurring in cyberspace ... but I think the analogy still holds.

We have to develop an educated consciousness that can cope with the technological outcomes of our playful imaginations. We have to be able to sift through those systems that empower and enrich our sense of agency (and if possible, proactively design these), and those which make us passive, dissatisfied, fruitlessly envious.

*The power of play*

This imperative is most acute in the case of the computer-games industry - an incredibly powerful tool for literacy, enabling the disciplined imagining and simulation of possible futures. However, in terms of content, games are currently trapped at the level of the penny-dreadful and the sensationalist novel - or worse, as in the case of the US Army, used as a scarily congruent recruiting tool. Yet the play-ethical response to games should not be one that demonises the play-form itself, but a concerted effort by the humanities and institutions of education to provide a non-commercial space for the development of alternative contents and uses.

What's extraordinary about the play-space of cyberculture is that it has, quite spontaneously and emergently, returned some very familiar old values back to the mainstream: the idea of a commonwealth, or what Lawrence Lessig in *The Future of Ideas* (Vintage 2002) would call an 'innovation' or 'creative commons'; the growth of active citizenship and reportage (see the rise of blogging and 'smart mob' street movements, nowhere more evident than in the Parisian demonstrations); and the emergence of co-operative organisational structures (see any number of activist, friendship or affinity networks).

> 'cyber culture is deeply congruent with the notion of play as possibility generator, helping us to thrive by generating options'

These values, emerging from within this play-space, stand alongside critiques of modernity coming from environmentalism, feminism or spiritualism - and indeed, in their horizontal and connective principles, have a deep affinity with them. Our elemental capacity for play, and the structures of the Net, have conjoined with startling fruitfulness at the end of the twnetieth century and the beginning of the twenty-first.

## Precarious life, flexicurity and care

I'd like to conclude by looking at the top-down political response to the prospect of a mainstream of player-citizens, player-consumers and player-producers. The political response has often been confused and contradictory.

Certainly the basic contradiction in most western societies - i.e. legislating for a full-on, capitalistic popular culture, with our visual environment strewn with mind-blowing and seductive advertising images in every corner, and then bemoaning the fact that 'dole bludgers' and 'sickie merchants' can't manifest enough commitment to their humdrum office tasks - is never addressed, or, it seems, even understood. There has been some shift in the direction of acknowledging common parenting rights for men and women - in which the classic (and ludic) test moment is the flexibility to able to see a daughter or son's school team play a mid-week match. Yet this has not been anywhere near enough to really address growing anxieties about how children are developing in a two-parents-full-time-working society.

There could be a more thoughtful state response to the possibilities, as well as risks, of *precarité*. In France, millions of students and workers recently took to the streets to protest against the *precarité*, or precariousness, that new deregulations of the labour market held out for their lives. In Australia, laws pointing in a similar direction have also caused many heated column inches but, as far as I can tell, little storming of the barricades. The English equivalent to *precarité* is 'precariousness', but this doesn't quite capture it; a more unsettling, fearful insecurity is implied.

There is a prankster political movement in Italy that aims to create a new patron saint for the flexible, short-term, precarious worker, called Punto San Precario. San Precario can be seen in supermarkets in Milan, in full costume, laying a benediction upon the poor shelfstackers. This has given rise to a whole, semi-subterranean discussion about the condition of precarity in the modern workforce, and how this might well be an opportunity for a new collective movement.[1] Frenchi, part of the Milan activist group Chainworkers, defines precarity this way: 'the problem of precarity is when they call you at midnight in order to tell you "look, tomorrow you've gotta work" when you've already got plans to go to Lugano to visit your family'. Chainworkers are keen to distinguish their complaint from that of the old Fordist worker, looking for a secure existence tied to a respected craft or skill. There is an element of the short-term, freelance-worker's condition - that lack of commitment to any organisation - that they like and enjoy. Like so many in this mobile-phoned, cheap-flying, net-café-dwelling generation, mobility and new experience are largely what they crave, in a context of strong friendship connections.

Their challenge to just-in-time capitalism is this: if you only require my

---

1. See www.16beavergroup.org/mtarchive/archives/001800.php. For a useful overview of these debates, see Brett Neilson and Ned Rossiter, 'From Precarity to Precariousness and Back Again: Labour, Life and Unstable Networks', *Fibreculture*, Issue 5 www.journal.fibreculture.org/issue5/neilson_rossiter.html

labour and skills for a limited period of time, and for a specific task only, then in return the state must provide me with 'social flexicurity' - that is, a social security that empowers the flexible worker to control her own time, to receive part-time rates in exact proportion to a full-time wage, to receive the same social benefits as a full-time worker. Frenchi's quip about precarity almost perfectly evokes the 'caring' end of my play-care duality, mentioned earlier. This is a player who wants the time and space to develop his human relationships, valued as an activity intrinsically good in itself. He is prepared to accept part-time work as the means to that balanced life, but resists the idea of employers putting his part-time productivity at their beck and call.

If this is part of the understanding of the French students' protest about new employment laws, then I would suggest that they are not as regressive or petit-bourgeois in their concerns as some of the commentary has suggested. I see the basic scene of the play moment being enacted here again: young people willing and eager to live exploratory, unpredictable, possible lives - the lives of players - but unwilling to do so without a solid ground of play. Without some collective assurance, that is, that this free play does not end up leaving them vulnerable to attack or exploitation.

I agree with Richard Sennett at the end of *The New Culture of Capitalism*, when he concedes that our technology-driven economies and societies have moved us irrevocably away from the old organisations of the past. The 'new men and woman' of information capitalism, shaped by their net culture and experience, simply won't buy the work ethic any more - their lives are too speedy, mutable and transformative for all that. But Sennett argues that one of the things the state can do is to help these new players build a narrative in their lives - some sense that their player's moves build up to some accumulation of talent, status or experience, rather than just a series of disconnected episodes. His answer to that, similar to the Chainworkers, is to promote the status of part-time work, and support it through various income supplements, targeted benefits and tax breaks. His second suggestion is that greater opportunities for social usefulness, for care and mentoring should be provided by the state, deploying the part-time and the underemployed.

Player-workers, in their mobility and fleet-footedness, may slip the bonds of social duty - but they may also miss that sense of responsibility and neededness also. A clever state should provide those opportunities - and not just as an entreaty to free voluntary action, but one which might also provide some kind of financial or material incentive.

Again, that tandem is appearing: play and care, care and play; the desire to live an adapting life of possibility and openness - but also the expectation that this will take place upon a background of support and protection. No matter how this may look to someone standing in the newly industrialising towns of China or India, this structure of feeling is, I suggest, where many of us in the rich parts of the world are, in our hearts and minds. Not tied to a work ethic - but heading towards a play ethic. The issue of what we do with this cognitive and affective surfeit, in terms of our attitudes towards local and global progressive reform, is the most urgent political question.

*This essay is adapted from a keynote lecture given by Pat Kane at The Brisbane Festival of Ideas, 2006.*

*For more ideas from Pat Kane go to www.theplayethic.com; or http://theplayethic.typepad.com*

# Musical jihad

## Amir Saeed

*Amir Saeed looks at cultural diasporas of hip-hop, Islam and black nationalism.*

Malcolm X preaching booms out of the loudspeakers: 'Our religion teaches us to be intelligent, be peaceful, be courteous, respect the law ... but if anyone puts their hands on you send them to the cemetery.' Three male figures, two clad in PLO headscarfs with only their eyes visible, suddenly appear to chants of Allah Akbar (God is Great), accompanied by heavy drums and hip-hop beats. My heart starts racing. Suddenly it's cool to be Asian, it's hip to be Muslim. The predominantly white crowd appear to appreciate and empathise with the politics.

This was my first encounter with British Muslim hip-hop pioneers Fun^Da^Mental. All my frustrations, anger and sense of helplessness were suddenly personified before my eyes, translated into a medium that my white peers could relate to. Before that, it had been cool to be black in popular culture, but no-one had wanted to be a 'paki'.

Fun^Da^Mental were a new experience, but hip-hop music had been entertaining and educating me for some time, and influencing my political outlook. Hip-hop, like Islam, is global and multi-ethnic. And, also like Islam, it is frequently misunderstood and misrepresented. This article explores the rise of hip-hop music as a global expression of youth culture; and it looks at its early relationship with Islam in the US, and the migration of this relationship across the Atlantic to Europe.

### The origins

Political hip-hop is at the heart of a developing global youth culture that combines influences from Arab, Islamic, black and Hispanic cultures, both local and diasporic. Together these are generating a hybrid revolutionary black, Asian and Hispanic globalisation movement that is challenging global imperialism. Pan-Africanism and pan-Islamism have been combined in a number of ways by African-American and Muslim intellectuals over the course of the last century as part of the fight against colonialism, racism and Western imperialism. And contemporary urban youth have adopted and modified these revolutionary ideologies into a global popular musical form. The cultural power of Islam, Black Nationalism and hip-hop have created a passionate, brash counter-culture that has significant appeal amongst groups who feel disenfranchised and powerless.

Tricia Rose coined the term 'Black Noise' in her exploration of the genesis of hip-hop culture in the USA in the 1970s and 1980s. Reagonomics and the cultural hybridisation of the South Bronx led many black and Latino youth to create musical sound systems, dancing, rapping and even art that reflected their surroundings and voiced their aspirations and fears. Within a decade researchers had articulated an 'Asian Noise', which addressed the booming British Asian dance music scene, which was heavily influenced by hip-hop culture. It now may be possible to expand on this further and talk about a 'Universal' or 'Global noise'. Hip-hop culture is now a dominant art form in youth culture, with a presence in countries as diverse as Egypt, Brazil, Japan, Australia, South Africa, Germany, Senegal, Algeria, Palestine, France, Cuba, China, Norway, Columbia and Mexico. Contrary to neo-orientalist discourses of an 'West-East' clash of civilisations, hip-hop culture has always been an amalgamation of cultures. In this respect Islam has had a tremendous influence on hip-hop from its beginnings. Many pioneer rappers, such as Afrika Bambaataa, belonged to Islamist organisations, and paid homage to Malcolm X, the Nation of Islam and Muhammad Ali.

By the end of the 1960s the growing political awareness that resulted from the civil rights and black consciousness movements was being articulated by increasing numbers of black performers in their music. From Sam Cooke's 'A Change is Gonna Come' to Nina Simone's 'Mississippi Goddam', black music articulated the dreams and fears of a generation. And as well the melodic harmonies of crossover black music, there was drum-driven, hard-edged funk, aimed at a blacker audience. These developments helped to sow the seeds of hip-hop, which borrowed or sampled extensively from the funk era.

Central to hip-hop culture is the creating of a descriptive narrative of life. It is a medium that conveys the aspirations and frustrations of the rappers. Chuck D of Public Enemy once noted that rap music was 'black folk's CNN'. An example is GrandMaster Melle Mels' 1982 song 'The Message' which chronicled ghetto life in the 1970s and 1980s, punctuated with its chorus 'Don't push me, cause I'm close to the edge'.

From the beginning, the relationship between Islam and hip-hop seemed natural, particularly in the USA, and many commentators have argued that Islam is hip-hop's official religion. The Nation of Islam (NOI) set up the 'Hip-Hop Mission' as a way of communicating with inner city youth. Louis Farrakhan delivered the keynote address at the 2002 Hip Hop Summit in New York City: 'Rap has brought the children of the world to you'. He noted that young people in the streets were being raised by hip-hop and their peers. Prominent US rappers like Public Enemy and Ice Cube were strongly connected to the NOI. The 5 Percenters, a group that broke away from the Nation of Islam, were also committed to attracting youth, with their mix of Islamist terminology and a Black Nationalist theology. Less strict in terms of dress and discipline than the NOI, the 5 Percenters proved to be a magnet for young black males, and the cultural language of hip-hop helped further expand their message. A number of prominent artists - such as Lakim Shabazz, The Poor Righteous Teachers and Rakim - had strong links with the 5 Percenters. Whilst none of these artists were orthodox Muslims, and all preached African-American/Black versions of Islam, they were an inspiration to 'mainstream Muslims' worldwide, especially Muslim minority communities in the West.

## Hip-hop ummah

Just as the African-American civil rights movement provided inspiration for oppressed people globally, the 'hip-hop generation' in the US has become a 'global hip-hop generation'. Since the events of 11 September 2001, Western interest in and fear of Muslims worldwide has become almost institutionalised in media and society. One consequence has been an increased assertion of Islamic identity by Muslims, who feel that their religion, culture and beliefs are under ever-increasing scrutiny. This assertion is embodied in the cultural field through Muslim hip-hop artists building transnational alliances, helping to develop what Samy Alim calls a 'hip-hop ummah'. Alim is combining the Islamic notion of the worldwide community with a global youth culture. It is also evident that the social and political factors which helped ferment hip-hop culture can be found in many Muslim minority communities throughout Western Europe. Muslims suffer poor housing, poor health and high levels of unemployment, and these socio-economic conditions have helped to generate Muslim hip-hop.

It is only recently that British-Asian hip-hop groups have managed to enter the mainstream, however, and even now this breakthrough is fairly limited. Some have used this platform to raise awareness about issues of racism: the last few years have seen the rise of bands like Black Star Liner (named after one of Marcus Garvey's organisations), White Town (named after the designated all white cities of South Africa), Cornershop (a tongue in cheek reference to the stereotype of Asian shopkeepers) and Asian Dub Foundation (ADF), whose name and music is intensely political.

Fun^Da^Mental are one of the key advocates of British Muslim political identity. Their name conjures up stereotypes of fundamentalist Islam, and their physical presence is further emboldened by PLO headscarves. Their rhetorical style has been likened to that of Public Enemy. Their music joins political dissent to a mix of hip-hop beats, Asian wails and African drumbeats, to create what the band calls 'Global Chaos'. Their raps combine homages to the Nation of Islam with samples of the Black Panther Party and orthodox Islamic leaders. The fact that at times the philosophies of these organisations might be contradictory appears not to be an issue. Fun^Da^Mental are attempting to highlight issues of oppression and racism, and they are willing to employ a Malcolm X inspired ideology of 'any means necessary' to underline their cause(s). In some respects they have adopted a politicised and aggressive Black, pan Islamic identity:

> So I'll be coming around the mountain
> With my Islamic warriors
> Nubians with Jihad on my mind
>     Fun^Da^Mental, 'Mera Mazab', 1994

Their song 'Dog-Tribe' was released after the BNP had won a council seat in East London, and recorded racist crime was at an all time high. The video, depicting an Asian youth beaten up by white racists, was banned on the grounds that it was too violent. The lyrics themselves openly called for self-defence.

The combination of a more local cultural and political assertiveness with global alliances and/or an 'Ummah politics' is expressed by a number

*Musical jihad*

of current Muslim hip-hop artists. Mecca2Medina have argued that hip-hop can harness and channel the frustration and anger of youth into conscious songs. London-based Blakstone share a similar perspective: 'Hip-hop is not Dawah (a call to prayer) but when it is used as a rally cry it touches the youth, our youth from places the Imams can't reach or fear to tread'. The group address the Iraq War, the Gaza Strip and corrupt dictators in Asia and Africa. They also encourage a positive Deen (way of life) for Muslim youth living in the West. For Blakstone, hip-hop can be used to bring back into the fold Muslim youth who are moving away from Islam. It can give Muslim youth an education in an entertaining format that will raise their awareness and self-esteem: 'We do not believe in compromise or violence. We believe that a way out is to concentrate our efforts in re-establishing a home for Islam. A place where Islam comes before race. Before colour, before nationality and before language.'

This international outlook of Muslim hip-hop seems inherent in Muslim groups globally. As in Britain, Muslims in France have taken the brunt of white xenophobia, islamophobia and racism; and the disturbances there in 2005 re-ignited debates about immigration and 'culture clash'. However, hip-hop seems to offer a bridge that can connect youths of diverse backgrounds without diluting its political message. The French group IAM (Imperial Asiatic Men) adopt the Black Nationalist colours of red, black and green alongside Islam's star and crescent. Again, the group is multi-ethnic and multi-racial - one of their rappers is an Italian convert to Islam. IAM openly acknowledge the influence of Islam in their music:

> Allah Akbar [God is Great] protect us from darkness
> Like King Raz said to whom I say salaam [peace]
> Ulemas [Islamic scholars] we are, souls of Islam.
> 'Red Black and Green', 1991

Throughout Europe, hip-hop groups have started to develop cross-over appeal. In Denmark the multi-racial group Outlandish furnish their songs with experiences of immigration. The group has members whose families originally come from Honduras, Morocco and Pakistan. A recent single 'Look into my Eyes' (2005) is based on a poem written by the Palestinian poet Gihad Ali:

Terror breathes the air I breathe
It's the checkpoint on my way to school
Terror is the robbery of my land
And the torture of my mother
The imprisonment of my innocent father
The bullet in my baby brother
The bulldozers and the tanks
The gases and the guns.
...
I'm terrorized in my own land
But am I the terrorist?

Outlandish have bridged the gap between subculture and mainstream popular culture, and achieved significant commercial success throughout Europe. And they have done this without forfeiting their politics. And they have also made a stand against militant Islam. They argued that the Muslim anger over the Danish cartoons, although justified, should have been channelled into dialogue with critics of Islam in order to combat ignorance and educate the Western world about Islam.

## Education through 'halal hip-hop'

Throughout Europe, Muslims are creating cultural, social and political spaces for themselves. They are at the forefront of anti-racist, anti-imperialist mobilisations. Hip-hop activism is an important cultural art form that is articulating Muslim opinion and helping to mobilise a cultural resistance to Islamophobia, at the same time as providing grounds for dialogue and understanding. For a disaffected young Muslim, Islamic hip-hop provides a vehicle of positive expression for his or her culture, while for the non-Muslim consumer hip-hop may be the only opportunity to encounter Islamic frustration or discover Islamic culture in an accessible, non-patronising manner.

Whilst the older generation of Muslims may not see a connection with Islam and hip-hop, this convergence for many Muslim artists seems almost 'natural'. The Holy Koran (which many scholars see as a collection of poems) was revealed to Prophet Muhammad (Peace Be Upon Him) orally, and in large sections through almost rhymed prose. It could be argued that this mirrors the vernacular linguistic pattern that is evident in hip-hop raps. The writer Abdel-Alim has interviewed a number of Muslim hip-hop artists who detail the similarities in hip-hop language and the text of the Koran. Mos Def (a Sunni Muslim African-American and now Hollywood actor) notes: 'the reason that people are able to be *hafiz* [one who memorises the entire Koran through repetition and study] is because the entire Koran rhymes ... hip-hop has the ability to do that - on a poetic level.'

However there are differing views in this area. Islamic community elders in Bradford were unhappy with Fun^Da^Mental's chanting of Koranic phrases over dance beats. For orthodox Muslims this is considered *haram* (forbidden). Theologians have been addressing the issue of Islam and music for centuries, and mainstream authorities note that music is permissible if it serves 'good purposes'. One can also see the influence in Sufi Islam of devotional Qawwali music, embodied in the songs of artists such as the late Nusret Fateh Ali Khan. However a more conservative view is that music is essentially a regressive force because it can excite passion and incite lust. Furthermore mainstream hip-hop has a negative image for Muslims: it is possible that Islam and hip-hop can be in contradiction, with one attempting to lead towards enlightenment and purity and the other towards the enjoyments of consumption, consumerism and commercialism.

## Hip-hop, Islam and moral panic

The current western media representation of Islam invokes discourses of violence and despotism. Ironically these are the same images that are promoted by corporate companies when marketing 'gangsta rap'. Whilst gangsta rap focuses on consumption and employs racist, sexist, homophobic and violent imagery, it can be argued that this genre has been manipulated by corporate interests into reflecting the prevailing values sustained by white supremacist capitalist patriarchy. Images of black youth as gang members fulfil white stereotypes of what black youth is. Young African-Americans then adopt these images themselves. The emphasis on consumption and bling culture has diluted the political potential of hip-hop. (Interestingly, the criticism of being sexist is often levelled - and with some reason - at both gangsta rap and Islam.)

A number of Muslim rappers have noted that hip-hop music today is plagued by *jahili*, an Arabic term that refers to the pagan age in Arabia before

Islam and generally denotes ignorance. Contemporary hip-hop has been marred by violence and disputes, which have contributed to the deaths of people like Tupac Shakur and Biggie Smalls, and it has a heavy disrespect of women and a sense of materialism that borders on jahili idol worship. The current fascination of mainstream American and global popular culture with violent gangsta rap parallels the neo-orientalist discourse that Islam itself is intrinsically violent or misguided. In both cases a process of demonisation is going on. Consider for example some of the burgeoning alarmist post-9/11 literature. Books like Bernard Lewis's *The Crisis of Islam*, Robert Spencer's *Islam Unveiled, Disturbing Questions about the World's Fastest Growing Religion*, and Serge Trifkovic's *Sword of the Prophet* rely on ambiguous categories such as 'Western civilisation'. This growing body of literature caricatures Islam and Muslims, and distorts Islamic concepts such as Jihad, which has come to mean 'holy war'.

The language of Islam in the culture of hip-hop does often express anger at western governments' foreign policy and indifference. East Bay rapper Paris deliberately used the word jihad in his most recent album *Sonic Jihad* to express frustration and rage at the current War on Terrorism. A militant Islam has been produced which promotes a more violent conception of jihad (struggle). A recent release by Sheikh Terra and Soul Salah Crew called 'Dirty Kuffar' (unbeliever) praises the attack on the World Trade Centre. It is accompanied by a video (available only online) that shows a young rapper brandishing a gun and the holy Koran. Whilst on the surface it seems that all these artists are anti-Western imperialists, their frustration is expressed in differing political ideologies. Paris's mix of Sunni Islam, Black Nationalism and anti-capitalism seeks to build alliances with other disenfranchised groups. Sheikh Terra's seems to be anti-Western *tout court*.

Should we be surprised by these differences? Islam itself is a multi-ethnic, multi-racial and multi-cultural melting pot. Varying histories of imperialism further complicate these elements. Diaspora Islam is not homogeneous, despite simplistic Western media depictions. These differences can manifest themselves in all aspects of Islamic culture, including youth culture. In short Islamic hip-hop covers the full spectrum of political ideologies, from left to right. Within the world of Islamic hip-hop, just as in mainstream hip-hop, contradictions and debates rage. Some artists are actively employing this

Western musical art form to communicate, open dialogue, and debate with wider society. Others seem to be exploiting the popularity of hip-hop to silence or terminate any dialogue with the West.

Politicians and Muslim leaders are now acknowledging the value of hip-hop in engaging with those who feel alienated and marginalised, though there are many questions about the future direction this culture might take. Hip-hop, the traditional music of the marginal, may help incorporate young Muslims in to the mainstream. This does not necessarily imply an assimilation or dilution of Islam, but rather a re-formulation of identity in a rapidly globalising world. At the moment this identity is still in its infancy and may manifest itself in contradictory fashion, but the passion and fire in much of Islamic hip-hop cannot be doubted. Adisa Banjoko, an African-American convert to Islam, in his recent book *Lyrical Swords: Hip Hop and Politics in the Mix*, writes: 'Hip Hop should not be feared ... it needs to be authentically researched, understood, appreciated, and discussed'. The same can also be said of Islam.

*Useful links for Muslim Hip-hop*
www.muslimhiphop.com/
    Useful link that has downloadable songs and tracks. It is also possible to search name of specific artist and hear samples of music.
youth.ibn.net/music
    Muslim web page that features link to songs by Muslim artists including hip-hop.
www.finalcall.com/
    Nation of Islam's online paper that has a link to its Hip-Hop Mission.

*Specific Artists*
www.guerillafunk.com
    Web page for Oakland rapper Paris, formerly of the Nation of Islam, which features links to Public Enemy and a multitude of radical political information, including readings on Chomsky.
www.fun-da-mental.co.uk
    Original British Muslim group with links to politics as well as music.
www.blakstone.com/
    UK based group which features links to music, video and Islamic history.
www.mecca2medina.com/
    UK based group which features the call to prayer on the web link.
www.mosdefmusic.com/
    Probably the most successful Sunni Muslim artist in the world.
www.sonsofhagar.com
    Seattle based Muslim group which features Palestinian-Americans.

# Late capitalist nights

## Jonathan Keane

*Can we escape the emotional terrors of the market invasion of our lives?*

My mum recently had a heart attack. She's well now though - the NHS working for her as one hopes it would, from state-of-the-art care in a new cardiac ward to rehabilitation in a keep-fit club down at the local gym. Gradually, she's getting her confidence back. When the first phone call came, my world and that of my brother and sister were thrown into shocking relief, of course. Our mum. It is at times like this when you need everything to work. My last boyfriend met me at the train station, putting aside the emotional pain of our long-running break-up. Love and support was what was needed now. Even Virgin Trains, with its fast and frequent west coast service, suddenly seemed God-sent. My brother's partner picked me up in the car. My family were all doing what each of us were best at to come to my mother's aid. We weren't all capable of every aspect of love and care, but what we could do we did, and we did it together. We became our best selves. It was a terrifying situation but one that allowed us all to be seen by each other, our relationships coming into view, both the good, and the aspects that needed a little work. Things were said. Life was lived.

**Wounds**
My mum shares a preoccupation with much of western culture right now (honest mum, you do). Repeatedly unsure, she is preoccupied with how her body works, of what's happening to it, how it will cope with all the future will bring. Though luckily for her, she knows exactly what has happened and, not accidentally, has a great deal of information and love to draw upon to decide how to proceed.

*Late capitalist nights*

Unfortunately, it seems most individuals and indeed national governments make do without like support. We seem to be experiencing regular shocks that are unfathomable, almost uncanny, with few ideas about what is happening or how to calm the situation down and move on. Events as apparently unconnected and various as acts of terrorism, dramatic rises in housing costs, the lights turning out in California, or signs forbidding dancing in New York, friends inexplicably not answering the phone, a young black boy being murdered in a miserable high-rise stairwell.

I often hear people saying they find things too 'big' or they feel too 'full'; that they don't have the time to respond or to 'fit things in'. Then there are the small admissions that leak out over a pint, of being on anti-depressants, of having a drink problem, of seeing a counsellor, of being in massive debt, or of not being able to get on trains; generally, of not coping or feeling on the edge. Equally random are those transitory moments when people feel great: they've just been given work, or found a moment of real clarity; someone has asked them out or likes their trainers. And friends constantly restate those moments, or what they like about each other and the places they live, as if everything will have changed a week or even a day later. People are stretched, on their uppers, manic and depressed, caught in the feedback of their own lives. This is a shared emotional landscape, in Britain especially, in which things seem to happen out of the blue, firing at us without warning in salvoes from all manner of directions. When we react, it feels awkwardly inappropriate. Our feelings are frequently returned with incomprehension or indifference from others who are in their own little reactive space. When we think we've got it, others think they're lost, and back again. At times it is literally overwhelming. My mum used to tell me I needed to toughen up.

A gifted and intelligent artist in London called Richard Squires has created the perfect figure for such times. Salivadriver is an interactive art piece involving a web cam scenario. Within it Richard plays an animated character who boasts a bruised eye due, we are told, to a recent trans orbital lobotomy. On the side of his face there is an exposed salivary gland. Viewers sit down and click on screen icons that can either stimulate Richard and make him salivate, or else anaesthetise him into sleep. A creeping sense of unease and abuse settles on your chest as you fiddle with this poor man on screen. In one sense it is a witty swipe at the brain-dead and emotionally removed activity of cruising and selecting someone on an internet dating site (as if people were chops in a butcher's window). But Salivadriver also points to something more disturbing. It made me think of events tweaking our buttons as if we are simply bundles of unreasoning tissue and fluid. As if victim to outside forces, we have a creeping sense that our capacity to think, our culture and emotions are being taken away or discarded. So much so that we can only respond by falling away into brain-damaged dormancy or silent dribbling. Unsurprisingly, lots of viewers didn't take to it.

Our society is overcrowded with symptoms of this eerie sense of free falling. Often I hear new mothers, for instance, speak of feeling they are bad at the job. They have got involved in Sure Start, gone to work, moved to an area with a good school, watched every episode of Supernanny, given up smoking and do yoga every day at 6am. But even when the evidence of their brilliant children declares the opposite, they persist in their guilt that they're not on the right track. And our children feel like they are failing all the time at school, even though they are getting the best results ever, more of them are going to university and they are the most issue-based and artistically creative generation we have ever had. They still feel isolated, feel they still need to do more, still hate their bodies and burn out at least once before they are eighteen.

In the film *L'Enfant*, the winner of 2005's Palme D'Or at Cannes, a man wheels and deals in the underbelly of French society to provide the gifts he thinks his girlfriend loves him for. When she goes to hospital to have a baby, he rents her flat to get her a car and jacket. When she has their baby, he follows the same entrepreneurial logic and sells the child for adoption. Quids in, he thinks she will be pleased. In the face of an action so clear and yet so awful, she malfunctions. Her eyes roll to the back of her head and she falls to the ground. At the end of the film, with the baby rescued, the mistake rectified, but the man now finding himself in prison, the two look at each other over a table and all they can do is cry. Heart-rending, body-shaking tears, expressive of so much that words simply cannot say. Their grief over a world in which they have tried to make their way but in which they have so terribly, unfathomably failed.

## Grief

When I was about eleven, I remember seeing the poster for the film Alien outside my local cinema. It was of an egg breaking open, letting out a slither of green light, and I felt both over excited and just a little frightened. Back then,

*Late capitalist nights*

the cinema came equal top in my list of the most exciting places in town, the other attraction being the revolving doors at the library, which as well as giving good spin, gave out strange smells of polish and old books. Both places promised magical and mysterious adventures once inside. Soon after, the cinema closed down and was razed to the ground, a bleak car park erected in its place. It was tragic. I felt like the magic had been ripped out of our town, never to return. For the first time, life felt randomly unfair.

It was the early 1980s of course, and unemployment in Widnes, my hometown, had soared from 2700 people in the spring of 1979 to 10,000 by the summer of 1983. People just didn't have the money to go out. But in many ways there was enough lively action going on outside the cinema to compensate. A legion of unemployed - by 1981 one and a half million in the North West alone - walking around aimless like the undead from a George A. Romero zombie flick. My town became a place where there was nothing to do and nowhere to go. I remember friends being frequently upset and weird, their homes strange and scary, inhabited for the most part by melancholic and angry adults. I remember plenty of arguments; teenagers having sex and sometimes babies; feeling unsafe; and gangs in graveyards digging up skulls. Indeed, as the South boomed the rest of Britain went Gothic. Some families fell apart, and whole generations felt their values, lifestyles and sense of identity were being purposefully attacked.

There were immediate casualties. Distressed school friends who went away to university simply to escape, only to find they were emotionally ill equipped to cope with the stresses and strains when they arrived. Misunderstood by self-confident, largely public school teenagers from wealthy southern families, they felt they didn't belong. Indeed, some had breakdowns and returned home. Those not lucky enough to get away were pressed into worthless Youth Training Schemes; working the cash till for our local Kwik Save, or on a building site, for £30 a week, with no hope of a career. Emotional damage always has a history and a politics. Likewise, it takes time and political vision to heal such deep wounds. The media snorted sarcastically at the jaunty New Labour 1997 election theme tune 'Things can only get better'. But it spoke to a country that deeply believed things really couldn't get any worse.

## Stories

Tommy Lee Jones's wonderful directorial debut, *The Three Burials of Melquiades*

*Estrada*, is a brilliant little fable about the almost impossible effort it takes to come to terms with such profound hurt. Jones plays Pete Perkins, a tough rancher who befriends Melquiades Estrada, an illegal Mexican immigrant who is accidentally shot and killed by a Texas border patrolman. Racist officials bury the murdered man with a careless lack of ceremony. Enraged, Perkins kidnaps the patrolman and makes him dig the body up. With only a picture of Estrada's wife for company, they set off into the desert, to fulfil a promise to return him home to be buried near his family. Days pass and Perkins looks after the corpse, combs its hair, and burns ants off his face, talking to him as if he still lives. Meanwhile the body of Melquiades Estrada blackens, decomposes, and gruesomely rots. When they finally reach their destination, it is to discover Estrada's fabled beautiful home does not exist and the woman in the picture is not his wife. But Perkins will not relinquish the story about his life his friend has so clearly fabricated. They settle on one arbitrary barren spot, define it as the man's home and bury him there, for good.

It is the sheer power of a story to shape our actions and help us work through grief that so powerfully animates this film. There is a subtle warning here too. If we, like the rancher, are forced to create stories on our own, and society fails to help, this can send our lives into irredeemable spirals of anguish. The cost of releasing grief in such circumstances is never insubstantial. Jones's character can never return home. He has made of himself an outcast.

In many ways we feel the Blair government has acted like the Texas border patrolman and the cold, unfeeling officials who helped bury Estrada's body. It was deaf to the anger we felt at the injustices of the Thatcher and Major years. But you can imagine just how powerful and believable a story Labour needed to tell in 1997 to stop every one of us heading down our own lonesome track. It wasn't just one death we needed to grieve, but countless rejections, arguments, separations (and for some families, suicides), all needing to be recognised, grieved, and, in their own way, buried out of sight.

Our disappointment feels all the more deep because when Tony Blair was first elected, it seemed he instinctively know the right words to say. We needed a big cry, which you could say we got when Diana, his 'people's princess', died. Yet, despite the beginning of what felt like a more socially humane era, something hindered and abruptly put paid to the prime minister's fabled 'new dawn'. It turned out New Labour's stories just didn't hit the mark. A generalised sense of uncertainty and depression not only remains, but seems to have increased, spread, and become more inchoate.

## Hate

Some answers lie perhaps in the wreckage of Labour's eighteen years in the political wilderness. During this time, the party tore itself apart in an orgy of self-hatred and infighting. Sets of values were casually discarded following each battle, from nuclear disarmament one year to taxing the rich the next. By the time Tony Blair came into power the party was almost unrecognisable. Where once they believed the market could do no right, now they believed, perversely, it could do no wrong. Indeed, to prove Labour's conversion, Gordon Brown embraced a never-ending revolution that insisted every sphere of society and culture be more productive and make more money, at lower costs. Investment in public services significantly increased and, to be fair, full employment, near enough, was achieved. But, as in Thatcher's time, we were still the major 'cost' that needed to be lowered. And so it is 'we' who have experienced the sharp edge of this whirlwind of productivity, from growing work pressures and insecurity, to feeling inept in the face of relentless change.

*'you can imagine just how powerful and believable a story Labour needed to stop everyone of us heading down our own lonesome track'*

In a sense, Labour's self hatred achieved something the Tories never dared: to raise free market economics up to a level of ineffable grace. The market mechanism is now beyond criticism and out of sight, accepted as a politically neutral tool of 'efficiency' without philosophical or emotional consequence. Consequently, market mechanisms have spread like a virus, adaptive, sublime and undefined, reaching deep into areas of our social and cultural life, radically changing how we live, in ways we simply don't have the knowledge to understand.

Under this regime, we have been subtly transformed from common people into managers of our own lives. Salesmen, touting our skills to prospective employers and administrators, bombarded daily with requests to decide between phone operators or gas suppliers, to calculate our own taxes, to skilfully renegotiate mortgages, even to decide who best to wield the surgeon's knife. Decisions (read 'choices') that for much of the twentieth century were made on our behalf, by people who knew what they were doing, and by institutions that, although inefficient, perhaps had our best interests at heart. Now, for the sake of efficiency, we are faced with impossible demands to be time-rich and productive urbanites, free of emotional baggage, or even emotional responses; to be tough and shiny, and exhibit angelic powers to adapt and bounce back.

It became impossible for Labour to talk through the market-inflicted pains of the Thatcher years: they would have had to admit they had been seduced by the very system that so tormented us. Their story of social justice, and indeed their achievements, parted company with our increasing sense of insecurity and sense of failing, anger and disappointment. Unemployment rates in Widnes returned to their 1979 level by 2003, but despite such signs that life was getting better, in the same year 19 million prescriptions were written for one antidepressant alone - Seroxat (Sarah Boseley, *Guardian*, May 13.5.06). Unlike Brown's productive angels, it seems we are made of more corruptible flesh and blood.

## Disgust

Beneath the shiny new hospitals, blue glass fronted-shops and countless house redecorations, we are not only ill at ease, we act as if carrying around, like Tommy Lee Jones, some morbid dead weight. Our stress and feelings of guilt and shame can, to some extent, be explained away by our failure to deal with the pressures of modern life. But what of the haunting sense of deathliness that seems also to possess and cling to our anxieties? Why do symptoms of compulsive and obsessive behaviour and complex addictions extend and proliferate? Why do increasing numbers of people take drugs like Ketamine - an anaesthetic that numbs emotions and pushes the world away - when they 'socialise'? And who or what is leading us into this strange, sensation-drenched world?

The producers of *Big Brother* are fond of boasting how people vote more for evictions on their show than they do for politicians. Perhaps this says less about the success of this freak show than how, in the absence of political understanding of our often brutal life, we turn increasingly to the mass media for explanation and distraction. Yet more than any other sphere, the media has been radically transformed by the extension of market values. Competition for advertising and ratings is intense, programmes are enlisted to shape audiences out of the insecurities we share, enticing fantasies are peddled as attractive lifestyle solutions.

*Late capitalist nights*

Our culture propels us into feelings of self-disgust. Countless TV programmes subtly and ruthlessly search out our fears of failing. Nasty little shows that delve into the houses of people who are filthy and don't clean and need routing out (*How Clean is Your House*). Or try to shame and cut fat, life-worn (and so disgusting) women into pristine and beautiful new beings (*Ten Years Younger*). And, surely top of the heap, *You Are What You Eat* - its central event a dominating tyrant of a presenter, Gillian McKeith, sniffing her victim's poo. According to the ads, it's 'Because we're worth it'.

## Horror

We are in thrall to a moving spectacle of self-punishment. Its cultural logic commandeers a captivating library of images we'd normally expect to find in horror films: humans being invaded or cut up, our bodies hiding alien impulses. We are brought back to life through a story-telling technique with echoes of Frankenstein and the Invasion of the Body Snatchers. All to animate what we're told is 'reality' TV. And we learn how we can solve our problems by obsessing over our bodies. But using horror stories to interpret neurotic symptoms - anorexia, bad debt, cleanliness obsessions, body dysmorphia and myriad addictions - only intensifies those symptoms. Our insecurities and fears thus lead us into dangerous, forbidding territory and there is no way out, even if you can afford surgery to completely change the way you look, change your whole diet, or buy a brand new shampoo.

Julia Kristeva suggests it may not be just what we watch on TV that is of concern: its seductive images make us daydream in a way that can only suspend, not alleviate, our anxieties and desires. The TV acts only as a screen for our feelings. There is no catharsis. If we look to it for help and solace, we experience, at best, a pleasurable disconnection. At worst we drown in images that give us no release, and begin to feel as if our own bodies are the enemy. We become increasingly (and shamefully) self-conscious, and frightened of the hungers, wants, fears and pains we wished to escape and that now seem to threaten us from within. Life can begin to feel truly nightmarish.

We seem to be turning into a culture of horror through which the self-punishing and wounding logic of the market enters our heads, declaring that our bodies are responsible for the failures the market increasingly inflicts on us - its consumerist fantasies of redemption intensifying, then suspending, then intensifying, our anxieties, in order that we can be exploited, over and over again. If this is so, we are all at risk of living in a state of dejection and without hope. Every aspect of our humanity, right down to our sense of what is real and not real, is now targeted and commodified, stripping us and our society of meaning and value. The empowering aspects of culture that tell us the stories we so dearly need to discover who we are and how we can belong are discarded in favour of more profitable fixes. A late capitalist night, deconstructing our identity, chunk by grisly chunk, until we have nothing left to give.

## Hope

When my mum got home from hospital she received nearly 100 cards and her house was a garden of flowers. She is an elder of a church and she had her heart attack when attending a meeting about how best to run a youth club. She trained to become a teacher during the early 1970s and has influenced many lives. Her first job was working in an office in a cigarette factory. She'd been told her five O-levels would never get her anywhere. Her dad was a proud French polisher, my Nan a housewife who used to read comics with me on the weekend. My dad had the same job from age 16 until retirement. So many people love and care for them both in their community (that's what I call respect), my mum eventually had to turn some away from visiting so she could get some rest. She is living a big and important life. The strong, emotionally subtle and complex community of which my mum is a part is no accident. She helped build it.

Thinking of them is heartening. What is happening to our society, though pretty horrific, is not, like the Matrix, a closed operation. It is not total or predestined. Rather a recent affront to a society that has a long, deep and well-connected tradition of human value. When my mum had a heart attack, we were all able to see that the NHS had got better, and that the trains were working. The failure of New Labour lies not here but in its failure to recognise that the economy it promotes to achieve improvements in the public services is ripping apart what people really care about: the fabric of our lives, what holds us together.

But there are some signs of people fighting back, and some recognition that the culture and politics that we are being served up are like amnesiac signs - pointing to something that seems familiar, but whose meaning we have somehow forgotten. And even when we are being targeted rather than supported by our culture, a very basic human need to relate sometimes bounces back in response.

We can't help it. Without it our sense of being dissolves. Although depression as a failsafe against the void can lead some to suicide, the majority get angry. In this sense, the seeds of failure of late night capitalism lie in the emotional lack at its core. Ultimately, we can't bear it.

It seems to me that the job of all of us that still feel we belong to the left is to reconnect with traditions that value relationships beyond the market and, in doing so, with each other. Not to 'modernise' values, but to bring humanist values into an increasingly inhuman setting. Once you decide to keep a critical distance from the market, then you can begin to tell a political story that connects with what people really feel. And the policy options that arise from this feel familiar, radical and above all supportive.

This would imply a refocusing of Labour values. Instead of seeing the property boom as an economic success story, we could think about it as a housing crisis that the market cannot solve, and recognise that the idea of social housing needs to be rehearsed once more. We could begin to rethink our social security system, and how it could be geared towards supporting people between the endless losing and regaining of contracts and jobs. To strengthen our cultural life, public institutions need to be reinvigorated and the logic of social value over monetary intelligently defended. To counter a culture of horror, questions of what is good public culture and what is the good society need to be asked, discussed and connected up, in a story of who we want to be.

Many young people are themselves building vibrant communities around bands, music, art, and new technology. They care about myriad political issues but are tribal and unsure in their futures. They need a political process that puts those issues above management of resources. And one that offers them education without the truly horrific price tag of debt. And we all need to assert that culture and art can be furthered and made outside of the wounding loop of market-led creativity. And if our lives feel isolated and scary, the answer lies partly in how we proceed personally. If we feel we cannot cope the answer isn't to watch TV, but to get out and talk to people. And if we're fearful of change, the answer isn't to blame foreigners, or even foreign criminals, but to read, talk and try to understand what is happening in our complicated, beautiful world. Making our own worlds of conviviality, thinking together and mutual help will be a big part of beginning the changes we need.

# Living inferiority

## Simon J. Charlesworth, Paul Gilfillan, Richard Wilkinson

*The authors show some of the ways in which living with inequality can damage the psyche.*

During the 1980s class differences in life expectancy widened dramatically in England and Wales. Figures from the ONS Longitudinal Study, based on a 1 per cent sample of the Census population, show that in the period 1972-6 life expectancy in Occupational Class I (professional occupations) was 5.5 years longer than in Occupational Class V (unskilled manual occupations) for men, and 5.3 years longer for women. By 1992-6 the class gap had widened to 9.5 years for men and 6.4 years for women.[1] Why did this happen?

We shall try to answer this question in terms of the social consequences of economic change during the period. An increasing body of research testifies to the importance to health of psychosocial risk factors which hinge particularly on the quality of the social environment and the health impact of chronic stress. These include factors such as social affiliations (both positive and negative), which range from close social support to involvement in community life, sense of control, hostility and social status. To illustrate the impact of these on people's lives we shall use excerpts from interviews gathered during a sociological study of working-class life in Rotherham in the later 1990s.[2]

Rotherham is a town in Britain's industrial Midland, which used to be heavily dependent on employment in coal mining and steel production. The severity of the social effects of the decline in the 1980s of employment in many of the

---

1. Office of National Statistics Longitudinal Study Press Release; and L. Hattersley, 'Trends in life expectancy by social class - an update', *Health Statistics Quarterly* 1999 2.
2. S.J. Charlesworth, *A Phenomenology of Working Class Experience*, Cambridge University Press 2000.

traditional heavy industries is often overlooked. The neoliberal economic policy of the 1980s and early 1990s undermined the foundations of the interpersonal forms of collective decency and solidaristic dispositions that once characterised industrial production and trade labourism in some occupational communities. It has transformed for the worse the way people relate to one another, and the way they perceive themselves. The most profound impact was on the quality of social relationships among the economically insecure. For them it fostered interpersonal conditions that promulgated anonymous forms of violence - against self and others - manifest in increased rates of violence and mental illness.[3] It can be argued that the neoliberal project aimed to create a world of constant competition which has resulted in a struggle of all against all, in which violence and cynicism often seem inevitable. As has been described elsewhere these new conditions have produced forms of social suffering which have led in turn to rising rates of violence, crime, drugs and alcoholism.[4] As one of Charlesworth's (2000) informants (a 29 year old wood machinist and father of six) explained:

> That's what it is, money. Money's quality, we can't offer that ... not only that, we are nice people, we can't afford to be nice, if we were nice out there, they look at it as a form of weakness, it's dog eat dog out there, we live in a fucking jungle man. You be nice out there, they think you're a fucking nerd, they do not recognise niceness, it isn't a fucking quality, niceness at our level is a weakness, you will not be respected for it ... that's why I just isolate myself, interact with fewer people.

Another man (57-year-old community worker, ex-steelworker and labourer) described it like this:

> They're all neurotic, all their thought processes are neurotic, in other words,

---

3. F. Flood-Page and J. Taylor (eds.), *Crime in England and Wales 2001/2002: supplementary volume*, Home Office Research Development and Statistics Directorate, London 2003; N. Singleton, R Bumpstead, M. O'Brien, A. Lee and H. Meltzer, *Psychiatric Morbidity among adults living in private households, 2000*, TSO, London 2001.
4. P. Bourdieu, *Pascalian Meditations*, Polity Press, Cambridge 2000; P. Gilfillan, 'Cardenden 1999: An Ethnography of Working Class Nationalism in a Scottish Village', Unpublished PhD thesis, University of Edinburgh 2002. See also Simon Charlesworth's A Phenomenology ... (see note 2).

things that you don't make clear decisions about - what's important and what's not important - everything, every crack, every time somebody looks at them funny, every time somebody says something to them they don't understand, it makes them worried and they respond in a worried way ... People say things to people. These days everything becomes a big issue ... in mental health terms: 'What did they mean by that?' People are more insecure ... they don't experience the world of work that gives them a base, it taught people how to live with each other and that it was important to get through work to know how to deal with people ...

Epidemiology has tended to focus both up-stream, on the social and material circumstance associated with poor health, and downstream, on the physiological effects of socioeconomic factors. Less attention has been paid to the intervening interpersonal and experiential processes that affect people. One of us has drawn attention to the need for a *'re-socialised* view of the human being', stressing the importance of the psychosocial effects of relative deprivation and suggesting that many of the biological processes that lead to illness are triggered by what we think and feel about our material and social circumstances.[5] What seems to be particularly injurious are those forms of interaction in which we feel 'put down' or degraded:

> Imputations of inferiority are highly aversive; and, even when it does not lead to violence, the sense of being put down or ignored generates strong feelings of angst in most of us ... To some extent we have become aware of these issues in the context of race and sex, but 'classism' remains rampant. [6]

The concept of the psychosocial is an attempt to recognise the primacy of emotional responses to human existence, particularly in relation to hierarchies of domination and subordination and how we intuit and respond to aspects of reality that are threatening to us. Discussions in this field often become polarised between material and psychosocial explanations for the basis of health

---

5. R.G. Wilkinson, *The Impact of Inequality: how to make sick societies healthier*, Routledge, London 2005.
6. R.G. Wilkinson, *Mind the Gap: Hierarchies, Health and Human Evolution*, Weidenfeld & Nicolson, London 2000, p28.

inequalities.[7] The latter seem to offer a difficult terrain to research before we have an adequate sense of how people manifest and perceive the negative evaluations of others. We also need to understand how resources are themselves constituted through relationships so that people evaluated negatively by others are often excluded from crucial resources.

The economic 'restructuring' of the 1980s resulted in widening income inequalities (particularly in the later 1980s), increased unemployment and a growth in the proportion of the population living in relative poverty. But if we are to understand why these changes had the particular social impact described in the interviews quoted above, we must understand the effects of social status and class differentiation.

> ... it's all around us. I went into social the other day ... there was ... a space next to this stuck up cow, you know, slim, attractive, middle class, and I didn't want to sit with her - you feel you shouldn't. I become all conscious of my weight, I felt overweight, I started sweating, I started bungling, shuffling. I just thought 'no, I'm not going to sit there. I don't want to put her out'. I don't want to feel that she's put out, you don't want to bother them ... you know you insult them ... the way they look at you like they're disgusted ... they look at you like you're invading their area ... you feel 'I shouldn't be there' ... it makes you not want to go out ... What it is, it's a form of violence ... it's like a barrier saying 'listen low life, don't even [*voice rises with pain and anger*] come near me! ...What the fuck are you doing in my space? ...We pay to get away from scum like you ...' It fucking stresses you. You get exhausted ... It's everywhere ... I mean, I clocked her like they clock us, right, and thought 'fuck me, I'm not even sitting there'. She would be uncomfortable, and it'll embarrass me ... [*voice rises in anger/pain.*] We were just sitting there, you know what I'm trying to say? ... It's like a common understanding, you know how they feel, *you feel it*, I'm telling you ... They are *fuck all*, they got nothing, but it's that air about them, you know, they've got the right, the body, the clothes, and everything, the confidence, the attitude ... We [*sadly, voice drops*] haven't got it, we can't have it. We walk

---

7. J.W. Lynch, G. Davey Smith, G.A. Kaplan, J.S. House, 'Income inequality and mortality: importance to health of individual income, psychosocial environment or material conditions', *British Medical Journal* 2000 320; M. Marmot, R.G. Wilkinson, 'Psychosocial and material pathways in the relation between income and health: a response to Lynch et al', *British Medical Journal* 2001 322.

in like we've been beaten ... dragging our feet when were walking in ... you feel like you want to hide ...

This comes from an unemployed man of 30 who ekes out his benefit by boxing on the burgeoning unofficial fight circuit. Why is it that, even without anything being said, just the perception of status differences can have such profoundly painful effects on people? Although we would argue that such effects are strongest and experienced most frequently by those nearer the bottom of the social hierarchy, feeling at a social disadvantage can have a powerful impact when people are 'outclassed' anywhere in society. A common theme in television sitcoms used to be the executive employee who had his boss to dinner and instantly became clumsy and incompetent, whatever he said heaping embarrassment on embarrassment. We all have a powerful capacity for shame and embarrassment. Indeed shame has been called '*the* social emotion', because it is through our fear of being seen as inferior or inadequate that we are rendered susceptible to the opinions and judgements of others, particularly to our social 'superiors'.[8] We may guess at how deep seated these processes are in our psychology from De Waal and Lanting's descriptions of ranking behaviour in chimpanzees.

> Chimpanzees go through elaborate rituals in which one individual communicates its status to the other. Particularly between adult males, one male will literally grovel in the dust, uttering panting grunts, while the other stands bipedally performing a mild intimidation display to make clear who ranks above whom.[9]

One of us has argued elsewhere that the areas where the most powerful psychosocial risk factors are found, such as social status, friendship and the social environment in early life, are important because of their bearing on our sensitivity to how we are seen by others (Richard Wilkinson, in *Impact of Inequality*). Early childhood experience gives rise to insecurities which feed into and are perhaps

---

8. T.J. Scheff, 'Shame and conformity: the deference-emotion system', *American Sociological Review* 1988 53.
9. F.B.M. de Waal, F. Lanting, *Bonobo: The Forgotten Ape*, University of California Press, Berkeley 1997, p30.

not unlike the insecurities of low social status. Both are associated with higher basal levels of cortisol (a central stress hormone) and a sense of low self-worth. In contrast, friendship tends to make us feel appreciated and valued: our friends find us interesting, attractive, good company. As reflexive beings, we know ourselves partly through the eyes of others: we monitor ourselves in relation to others and our experience of ourselves is therefore our imagined view of how others see us. This ability is clearly one of the foundations of human social life, and close to the core of what we mean when we call ourselves social beings. Negotiating social interaction and the public space can be a source of powerful social anxieties if we feel put at a social disadvantage, made to feel inferior, put down or disrespected.

These ideas resonate strongly with the work of social theorists working in the phenomenological tradition, such as Bourdieu. Contrast the sense of inferiority described above by the man in the Social Security office with what Bourdieu says about how the opposite feelings of value and self-worth are constituted:

> ... there is a happiness in activity which exceeds the visible profits ... which consists in the fact of emerging from indifference (or depression), being occupied, projected towards goals, and feeling oneself objectively, and therefore subjectively, endowed with a social mission. To be expected, solicited, overwhelmed with obligations and commitments is not only to be snatched from solitude or insignificance, but also to experience, in the most continuous and concrete way, the feeling of counting for others, being *important* for them, and therefore in oneself, and finding in the permanent plebiscite of testimonies of interest - requests, expectations, invitations - a kind of continuous justification for existing ...
> 
> But, to bring to light, perhaps less negatively and more convincingly, the effect of consecration, capable of rescuing one from the sense of the insignificance and contingency of an existence without necessity, one could, rereading Durkheim's *Suicide* ... observe that the propensity to commit suicide varies inversely with recognised social importance and that the more that agents are endowed with a consecrated social identity ... the more they are protected against a questioning of the sense of their existence ... The social world gives what is rarest, recognition, consideration, in other words, quite simply, reasons for being. It is capable of giving meaning to life ... One

of the most unequal of all distributions, and probably, in any case, the most cruel, is the distribution of symbolic capital, that is, of social importance and of reasons for living ... All the manifestations of social recognition which make up symbolic capital, all the forms of perceived being which make up a social being that is known, 'visible', famous, admired, invited, loved, etc, are so many manifestations of the grace (*charisma*) which saves those it touches from the distress of an existence without justification ...

Conversely, there is no worse deprivation, no worse privation, perhaps, than that of the losers in the symbolic struggle for recognition, for access to a socially recognised social being, in a word, to humanity (Bourdieu, *Pascalian Meditations*, pp240-2).

Bourdieu's mention of suicide is important in this context: suicides rose rapidly among young men from the mid-1980s - particularly among the unemployed. In this passage Bourdieu makes explicit that it is the conditions of people's feelings of worth and value - what amounts to their humanity - which is at stake.

Many of the changes that have taken place to the economic order have increased working-class people's exposure to situations in which they find themselves evaluated, judged and graded against formalised criteria. For example, as employers no longer needed young working-class people in such numbers after 1979, the route into employment changed radically. Until sometime in the 1970s a majority of school leavers went into employment in *relatively* well paid jobs with no qualifications.[10] That has now virtually ceased, and entrance to work is now mediated by a host of post-sixteen training and educational programmes so that even many manual workers go through some 'post-compulsory' education.

This is a crucial change in the experience of entrance to the labour market and in young people's chances of earning enough to support stable patterns of relationships. What we now have are conditions in which many more experience education, but the outcome is less certain and the experience is fraught with ambiguity. Many feel press-ganged into tertiary colleges as a condition of receiving state benefit, and have the experience of being forced to compete in

---

10. D.S. Byrne, 'Deindustrialization and Dispossession', *Sociology*, Vol. 29 1995; R. MacDonald, *Youth, the 'Underclass' and Social Exclusion*, Routledge, London 1997.

*Living inferiority*

conditions in which they are judged, informally as well as formally, for credentials they feel are worthless.

In Bourdieu's words:

> It is clear that children of the most culturally and economically disadvantaged families cannot gain access to the different parts of the school system, and to the higher levels in particular ... But it is just as clear that these students are directly responsible for the devaluation that results from the proliferation of degrees and degree-holders, meaning the new arrivals, who are its first victims. After an extended school career, which often entails considerable sacrifice, the most culturally disadvantaged run the risk of ending up with a devalued degree. If, as is more likely, they fail, they're relegated to what is undoubtedly a stigmatising and total exclusion even more absolute than in the past. The exclusion is more disgraceful in the sense that they seem to have 'had their chance' and because social identity tends more and more to be defined by the school system. And it is more absolute because a growing number of positions in the job market are customarily reserved for, and are in fact held by, ever growing numbers of degree-holders. This explains why, even in the lower classes, people see failure at school as catastrophic. So, to families as well as students, the school system increasingly seems like a mirage, the source of an immense, collective disappointment, a promised land which, like the horizon, recedes as one moves toward it.[11]

The experience of further education has become a central aspect of how working-class people come to experience judgements about their person and the kinds of social spaces they can enter. The following description shows the feelings generated. It comes from a working-class man going to his local university:

> It slowly grinds you down, mate, day in, day out, going in ... I drive in, and there's a certain point, a tree or a sign-post, and I'm 'right, this is where Uni starts'. I feel my stomach tighten, and inside it's all down hill from here, till I come back past that point and I'm like, 'right this where home starts, this is comfort zone'. I recognise it, that's where home starts, I recognise this

---

11. P. Bourdieu, *The Weight of the World*, Polity Press, Cambridge 2000, p423.

'I'm out of the Uni, I'm comfortable, I can cope'. That's why I drive back, even between my lectures, just to see those points, to get back and see the Woodman and think 'right, I'm OK'. You recognise landmarks, and it gives you that detachedness from Uni.

What matters is of course the treatment and forms of contact people feel they encounter. Here a man in his mid twenties describes his wife's experiences:

Our lass went to Uni ... did law. She can't get a job, she's down at Ventura [*a local call centre*], she fucking hates it ... She's given up looking for owt in law, she says you go in to interviews and it's like this [*imitates looking up and down with look of disgust*] ...You know she doesn't look like a slapper or nowt, she dresses nice, but she says when she goes in room, they look like this [*imitates again*] ...Our lass said she went to one interview, they had her waiting outside and she could see them through the window laughing at her ... I'd go fucking barmy, I can't deal with those people ... Our lass says it's just the same people from Uni all the time. She went for one, they rung her up and asked her to go along to interview, then when she walked in, the woman were like this [*again imitates looking up and down with judgmental disdain*] ... She were never there, she never mixed with those kinds of people, she stayed round here with her mates.

This vividly captures the non-verbal cues and sign-reading operations that are significant in personal encounters in which middle-class people discern the relative social significance and position of individuals. This testimony shows the uniformity of criteria of value that operate across educational and labour markets and make people feel excluded. The effects of the social hierarchy have become more profound and more personal. Working-class people experience more fully and more brutally the logic of the relations which constitute their social being: they exist as the repository of negative characteristics.

Working-class people confront this logic as it is played out in terms of different markets, for example when they try to get jobs, or in their experience of college situations, or informal social markets like pubs and night-clubs. They experience this logic in non-verbal cues showing they are not perceived as possessing the requisite social value. The greater involvement of manual workers in education

*Living inferiority*

and the extension of education only makes the logic of class more manifest.

We begin to see, on a personal level, why Bourdieu says that 'objective truth of ... position occupied in the school system, or in society, is never completely repressed ...' (*The Weight of the World*, p424), and why he is correct to say that 'the most personal is the most impersonal'. For those who lack the value to solicit engaged forms of concern, their experience of being a person is impersonal, because they lack the significance to be engaged with *personally*, in personal terms, so that being a person is not something they are habituated to, and they become accustomed to not really showing up as important in terms of key social markets. This is why Bourdieu goes on to say that many of 'the deepest malaises, the most singular suffering that ... [people] experience find their roots in the objective contradictions, constraints and double binds inscribed in the structures of the labour and housing markets, in the merciless sanctions of the school system, or in mechanisms of economic and social inheritance'.[12]

When working people say 'having nothing' is stressful, it is because it is linked to, and emerges from, an experience of being nothing, denied even self-respect. The way in which one unthinkingly carries one's body is an expression of one's social position, identity, and cultural background. So that how one opens a fridge, how one shuts a car door, how one smokes a cigarette, can manifest one's position as it has been insensibly internalised. Through the cultural appearances and 'body language' they exude, people are always radiating significances, exchanging sense, in a 'dialogue' of physiognomies. This is an inescapable condition of social contact. And the way in which middle-class people realise their own worth, and establish their claim to be worth noticing, uses elaborate and assertively instantiated symbolic forms of significance which are constituted in opposition to those of working-class people.

This is the real personal level of class. It is about enacted differences that gain their sense from the flow of practice and the cultural patterns of the public realm, and it is this which working-class people face. The following comes from a 25 year old design student:

> ... there's nothing you can do, what can you do: dress smart? If we dress smart

---

12. P. Bourdieu, and L.J.D. Wacquant, *An Invitation to Reflexive Sociology*, Polity Press, Cambridge 1992, p201.

> they'll spend a load of money dressing down, they'll spend a hundred and twenty quid on some retro-trainers, where we try and have the best we can afford, we're shown up by trying to look smart, they can see that money's not there. We buy a new jacket and think we got a fucking bargain, they spend twice as much on stuff that looks out of date ...

In everyday social encounters, significance emerges through uncodified, non-verbal gestures and symbols, as a covert indication of, and claim to, worth, position and entitlement. Through the patterns of their embodiment, people radiate significances and exercise their differential worth. In unequal societies, power exercised differentially through positive and negative values has an illicit political efficacy. Behavioural routines function as quasi-codes, and realisations of significance involve an allusion to the unworthiness of relevant others. Particular patterns are evaluated through the system of differences they 'refer' to, and the background of public intelligibility which is the condition of their being meaningful.

These forms are invested with power and fulfil quasi-political functions in that they are part of the exercise of what Bourdieu refers to as 'symbolic violence' in hierarchical and economically unequal societies. In these societies there is an imminent conflict running throughout public space which emerges from the physical, embodied marks and patterns of being that arise from economically disparate conditions of existence. What social epidemiology shows is that symbolic domination is difficult to resist because 'it is something you absorb like air'.[13]

> We learn bodily. The social order inscribes itself in bodies through this permanent confrontation, which may be more or less dramatic but is always largely marked by affectivity and, more precisely, by affective transactions with the environment ... it would be wrong to underestimate the pressure of oppression, continuous and often unnoticed, of the ordinary order of things, the conditionings imposed by the material conditions of existence, by the insidious injunctions and 'inert violence' (as Sartre puts it) of economic and social structures and of the mechanisms through which they are reproduced

---

13. P. Bourdieu and T. Eagleton, 'Doxa and Common Life', *New Left Review* 191, 1992, p115.

The most serious social injunctions are addressed not to the intellect but to the body, treated as a memory pad (*Pascalian Meditations*, p141).

The reach and affective power of these processes is shown in the following from a man in his late 30s whose work, connected with the Sheffield steel industry, involves travelling in Britain and Europe:

> I've lived in London, I know how they look at you, how they talk down to you. Fucking hell man ... I've felt better after a beating than how they tie you up, make you feel small, with their words, you can see it in those people - how they are. It's all of them, you see it's a war, there's us and them and they're hostile if we're in their space. They wouldn't physically beat you, but they'll make you feel even worse man. I'd rather have to fight somebody than that, at least you've got a chance like that.

This interpersonal experience of class is part of the way in which class relations are constituted and the class structure realised. Each class's experience of people in other classes is different and depends on how one is positioned in terms of relational significances, and how one is perceived in terms of the patterns of significance through which social relations are realised. Just as the police now accept that most racism is experienced non-verbally and have had to adopt a definition of racism as being anything that the person *felt* to *be* racist, regardless of the consciousness of the supposed perpetrator, the same can be said of classism and the processes of prejudice against those of lower social status - of which racism is a particular instance.

Bourdieu has spoken of the 'socially constituted agoraphobia' that leads people to 'exclude themselves from a whole range of public activities from which they are structurally excluded' (*Invitation to Reflexive Sociology*, p74). These forms of social exclusion not only impugn and degrade people's dignity, but also lead to extreme nervous tension and trigger stress responses rooted in people's sensitivity to their own negative significance. It is not surprising that involvement in community life seems to decrease as income inequalities - and so social distances - increase. Putnam showed that in the parts of the United States where involvement in community life was weakest (and where income differences were greatest), it was particularly the least well off who no longer participated in associational life.[14] The tendency for voter turnout in elections to decline where income differences are bigger may be part of the same phenomenon.[15]

Given the anger which imputations of inferiority and disrespect can cause, neither is it surprising that violent crime and homicide are robustly related to the scale of income inequality in a society.[16] Indeed, it was a prison psychiatrist of 25 years standing who said:

> I have yet to see a serious act of violence that was not provoked by the experience of feeling shamed and humiliated, disrespected and ridiculed, and that did not represent the attempt to prevent or undo this 'loss of face' - no matter how severe the punishment ... [17]

The scale of stress and anxiety which arises from people's constant daily insecurities and experience of social position affects health in two ways: first, it leads to increased reliance on the use of tobacco, alcohol and drugs, which provide at least temporary escape from stress; and second, chronic stress has direct physiological effects through the hypothalamic-pituatary-adrenal axis on both the cardiovascular and immune systems. Societies with bigger income differences are likely to have a bigger burden of relative deprivation, a more hierarchical social structure, and so also a greater burden of the forms of suffering we have described. Social processes of this kind are likely to contribute to the tendency for health standards to be lower in societies where income inequalities are larger.

*This article first appeared in The British Medical Bulletin Vol.69 2004, p49-60, and is reprinted by permission of Oxford University Press. We would like to thank Dr Kate Pickett and Dr Mary Shaw for giving their time generously to reading and making many helpful suggestions on earlier drafts of this paper.*

---

14. R.D. Putnam, *Bowling Alone: collapse and revival of American community*, Simon and Schuster, New York 2000.
15. T.A. Blakely, B.P. Kennedy, I. Kawachi, 'Socioeconomic inequality in voting participation and self-rated health', *American Journal of Public Health* 2001 91(1).
16. C.C. Hsieh, M.D. Pugh, 'Poverty, income inequality, and violent crime: a meta-analysis of recent aggregate data studies', *Criminal Justice Review* 18, 1993. See also Richard Wilkinson's *The Impact of Inequality*.
17. J.Gilligan, *Violence: Our Deadly Epidemic and its Causes*, G.P. Putnam, New York. 1996, p110.

# Prisons and how to get rid of them

## David Wilson

*David Wilson argues the urgent need for resistance to the massive increases in the prison population that are taking place under New Labour.*

Let me start by quoting from two different books, both published in 1990. The first is Labour Peer Baroness Blackstone's *Prisons and Penal Reform*, part of the *Counterblast* series published by Chatto and Windus at the height of Thatcherism:

> Britain has a disastrously expensive and inhumane penal system, which is compounded by a huge injection of resources into building more prisons. Placing so much emphasis on building prisons is a sad reflection on the innovative abilities of the government. A little more imagination, rather more attention to the evidence in front of them, and greater political courage would have led ministers down a quite different path. It would have led them to a sustained effort to reduce substantially the prison population.

That this was written some time before the days when New Labour would become 'tough on crime, and tough on the causes of crime' can be seen in Baroness Blackstone's call at the end of the book for the prison population be cut by half - to something around 24,000 people.

The second book is Norwegian criminologist Thomas Mathiesen's *Prison on Trial* (though it was published in 1990 I am quoting here from the second edition, re-issued in 2000). Mathiesen's position echoes Baroness Blackstone and optimistically predicts that *reason* will eventually persuade policy-makers that prison is illogical.

Victim work and offender work will certainly prove more satisfactory than prison, and we may envisage further contraction, possibly abolition. This would be congruent with the whole weight of evidence on prisons. In actual fact, anything else is tantamount to acceding towards irrationality.

Now, from our vantage point some sixteen years later, we can see that under New Labour there has been unparalleled growth in the penal system - since 1997, far from overseeing a fall in the prison population, New Labour has put around 30,000 extra people behind bars, and our prison population is currently at its highest ever level. As a result of their enthusiasm for mandatory minimum sentencing, there are now more Life Sentenced prisoners in Britain than in the whole of the rest of Western Europe combined. And furthermore, New Labour has presided over a greater amount of penal privatisation than their Tory predecessors, despite no less a person than Tony Blair himself once claiming that Labour opposed prison privatisation 'in theory as well as in practice'.[1] We also have the déjà vu experience of hearing our current Chief Inspector of Prisons echoing all of her predecessors in describing how awful the experience of incarceration actually is in this country.

No one, it would seem, would currently agree with Mathiesen that there might come a day when the contraction and eventual abolition of prison would become possible, and that to do otherwise would be 'irrational'.

Indeed 'common sense' justifications of prison suggest that prison 'works' in a number of ways: by incapacitation - it takes people out of society and thus gives communities a rest from those who have broken the law; through individual and general deterrence - it makes those who might be thinking about committing a crime think again; by punishing those who do actually commit crimes; and, finally, by rehabilitating - it helps those who have committed crimes to think through the causes of their offending so as to change their behaviour by developing new skills, which they are then able to put to good use on release from custody.

---

1. T. Blair, 'Address to the Perrie Lectures', Prison Service College, Newbold Revel 1993.

*Prisons and how to get rid of them*

These justifications are now so widespread and accepted amongst our politicians, media commentators and indeed many members of the public, that no one actually bothers to question whether they are actually true or not - whether they are 'nonsense' rather than 'common sense'. And the one place that we can forget about 'evidence-led practice' in relation to public policy is when prisons are discussed. After all, as a mountain of research testifies - much of it emanating from the Home Office - these justifications are at best aspirational and at worst simply lies.

Here it would be easy to unmask these false justifications by patiently pointing out the realities about who gets imprisoned and who does not; the relationship - or otherwise - between the crime rate and the rate of imprisonment; and what happens to people when they are inside - and, especially, what happens to them after they are released - in relation to the likelihood of their being reconvicted. We'd point to the fact that four out of every five young offenders are reconvicted within two years of leaving jail; that one out of every two adult men are similarly reconvicted; and, that just under one out of every two women suffer the same fate. Would a school that failed to teach two out of every three of its pupils to read and write, or a hospital that killed one out of every two of its patients continue to receive widespread political and popular support? However, we know all of this too. We know that prison fails by almost every measure that it sets for itself. We know that prison is a useless, outdated, bloated Victorian institution that is well past its sell-by-date. We know, in short, that prison is a fiasco. The problem is to try to change the common sense that refuses to recognise all this; to seek to create a scepticism about prison and the claims that are made for it by its supporters - that broad coalition of media commentators, big business and politicians of both parties whom we might term the 'prison-industrial complex'.

I want to make a case in support of Mathiesen from the perspective of describing the pre-conditions that have to be present for contraction and abolition to take place. For what I feel has been absent from this debate is a 'road map' of how we get from where we are to where we - or at least I and a number of prison abolitionists - would like to be. I absolutely agree that using prison is irrational, especially in relation to the numbers of people that we send inside, who, as all evidence shows, are largely minor property offenders who could be more effectively dealt with through community penalties, and I agree that prison is counter-productive, or to quote a former Tory minister, 'an expensive way of making bad people worse'. But we need more than these arguments; we need to show that it is possible to bring about the changes we seek. So, I want to draw on an historical example of decarceration, and analyse how that decarceration occurred, in the hope that this might guide us in our own attempts to stop the seemingly inexorable growth in prison numbers. (And here I note that I have been attempting to create this road map for some time, most recently in my book *Death at the Hands of the State*, which is published by the Howard League for Penal Reform, and which I hope can also be read within the honourable tradition of European penal abolitionism.[2])

In making this road map, I do not intend to discuss 'alternatives' to imprisonment - though this is a subject worthy of much greater consideration, for two reasons. Firstly, there are now many alternatives to imprisonment, both in the statutory and voluntary sectors, so that we have witnessed the phenomenon of the prison population increasing in tandem with the development and growth of these 'alternatives'. In short, we have what Stan Cohen described several years ago as 'net widening, and mesh thinning'.[3] By this process suitable candidates are found for prison and for the alternatives to prison. Secondly, given that this is so, what is really needed is for the debate to be shifted away from the question of 'alternatives' to imprisonment - which have increasingly been subsumed into the prison-industrial complex - to start discussion about the real alternative to imprisonment, which is of course decarceration and eventual abolition.

There are several historical examples of decarceration that I could choose. For example, there was a decline in prison numbers in the old West Germany in the 1980s, which for a time provided a great deal of hope for penal reformers in this country; and in the Netherlands between 1950 and 1975 the prison population fell from 6500 to 2500, despite an increasing crime rate. There was also a process of decarceration of young offender institutions in Massachusetts in the 1970s, under the leadership of Jerome Miller, during Michael Dukakis's tenure as State Governor.

Each of these examples offers some insight into the politics of decarceration.

---

2. D Wilson, *Death at the Hands of the State*, Howard League 2005.
3. S. Cohen, *Visions of Social Control*, Polity 1985.

For example, it is quite clear that Dukakis was seen as 'soft on crime' during the Presidential campaign of 1980, and that subsequent Democratic candidates - most notably Bill Clinton - were keen to establish their 'toughness' about offenders: many readers will remember the story of Clinton leaving the campaign trail in 1992 to return to Little Rock, Arkansas, in order to sign the death warrant of Ricky Ray Rector, a mentally disabled black man.

## Decarceration: an example from history

In fact I have chosen an example of decarceration from England and Wales, for it seems to me that the decline in the prison population of England and Wales between 1908 and 1939, from 22,029 to 11,086 - or in terms of the numbers of prisoners per 100,000 of the general population from 63 to 30 - was a truly extraordinary occurrence, and one that deserves greater scrutiny.[4] In effect, our prison numbers halved during this period, and as a result around twenty prisons had to close, despite the fact that the crime rate in this period actually increased by around 100 per cent. Let's look at these figures a little more clearly (see Table 1).

*Table 1 - Prison Population 1908-1938*

| Year | Total Prison Population | Rate per 100,000 |
|---|---|---|
| 1908 | 22,029 | 63 |
| 1913 | 18,155 | 50 |
| 1918 | 9196 | 25 |
| 1923 | 11,148 | 29 |
| 1928 | 11,109 | 28 |
| 1933 | 12,986 | 32 |
| 1938 | 11,086 | 30 |

*Source: Adapted from Rutherford's* Prisons and the Process of Justice

So how can this phenomenon be explained? I think there were three main factors. Firstly, there was a climate of scepticism at the time about what prison

---

4. This example has been written about by A. Rutherford, in *Prisons and the Process of Justice*, Oxford Paperbacks 1988.

and imprisonment could do, and it was shared by a wide range of people who were able to exercise influence over the political process. Secondly, there was a credible, practical alternative to incarceration, which was used by policy-makers, magistrates and judges as a genuine alternative. Thirdly, prisons and prison staff responded to this changing sensibility, both prompting and supporting the drop in prison numbers.

During this period a number of politicians and key social groups became absolutely convinced that prison was a corrupting and counter-productive experience. The most obvious example of this was Winston Churchill, who as Home Secretary between February 1910 and October 1911 set about reducing the use of imprisonment, especially for those who had hitherto been sentenced to very short sentences. He noted, for example, that in 1910 some two-thirds of sentenced prisoners had received sentences of two weeks or less, and he described this as 'a terrible and purposeless waste of public money and human character'. More famously, in July 1910 he also suggested that 'the mood and temper of the public to the treatment of crime and criminals is one of the most unfailing tests of the civilisation of the country'. Just why Churchill was so against prison is a matter of conjecture, but perhaps we can trace his antipathy back to his own experience as a prisoner-of-war during the Boer War, and it is worth noting that politicians who themselves have had direct experiences of incarceration - such as Nelson Mandela and Vaclav Havel - are usually the most ardent penal reformers when they come to power.

Churchill's scepticism was mirrored in this period by other key and influential groups and commentators, who created the right 'mood music' for decarceration to take place. For example, Oscar Wilde was arrested in 1895 on charges of gross indecency and sent to gaol for two years. Whilst inside he wrote *The Ballad of Reading Gaol* which had a tremendous popular impact when it was first published in 1898; as far as I am concerned it remains one of the best pieces of prison writing that Britain has ever produced. Similarly, the incarceration of suffragettes in the period immediately before the first world war, as well as their treatment inside, and the imprisonment of conscientious objectors during the war, created two powerful groups of people who were prepared to campaign for changes in relation to imprisonment. The most obvious example here is the formation of the Howard League for Penal Reform in 1921. Two conscientious objectors who had suffered imprisonment, Stephen Hobhouse and

Fenner Brockway, conclude in their in 1921 book about prisons that:

> Our prison system, whilst it sometimes makes good prisoners, does almost nothing to make good citizens. It fails to restore the weak will or to encourage initiative; it reduces energy by the harshness of its routine and adds depression to the depressed ... and the more the system costs the country, the more highly it is organised, the more monumental must that failure be.

The second development that I believe created the preconditions for decarceration in this period was the development a credible alternative to incarceration. Specifically it is during this period that we see the development of Probation. The roots of probation go back to 1876 and The Church of England Temperance Society, and by 1907 the government had passed its first Probation Act, giving probation a statutory footing. In short, by then imprisonment was not seen as the 'only club in the golf bag' of policy options when it came to responding to offenders, and this allowed the hegemony of incarceration to be challenged. Here, in passing, we should note that Probation was not subsumed by the prison system, but rather maintained its independence and difference.

The third factor was the response of the Home Office, prisons and prison staff to these changing social and policy developments. They were not the passive recipients of change, but rather both prompted and responded to it. Their response is perhaps best symbolised by The Gladstone Committee of 1898, which completely re-defined the purpose of imprisonment; for example, it stated that:

> We think that the system should be made more elastic, more capable of being adopted to the special cases of individual prisoners; that prison discipline and treatment should be more effectively designed to maintain, stimulate, or awaken the higher susceptibilities of prisoners, to develop their moral instincts, to train them in orderly and industrial habits, and whenever possible to turn them out of prison better men and women, both physically and morally, than when they came in.

These challenges were admirably taken up in prisons and prison staff, for example through the development of the borstal regime for young offenders, and the introduction of psychologists and educationalists into prison regimes.

## Campaigning for abolition

So, what lessons can we learn from this historical example about decarceration in our own day? - a time of not just record prison numbers, but also of the closer relationship between HM Prison Service and the National Probation Service, under the National Offender Management Service (NOMS) (and thus at a time when a credible alternative to imprisonment seems further away); a time when prison regimes are dominated by cognitive skills courses of various kinds, which seem to promise - on the sketchiest evidence available - that prison can in some circumstances be 'good for the offender'; and at a time when a seemingly never-ending procession of politicians are prepared to see the prison population grow higher and higher, ignoring a mountain of evidence about its ill effects.

The key lesson for me is that we have to re-create a sense of scepticism in the policy debate - a scepticism robust enough to transcend the party politics of the lowest common denominator, whilst at the same time creative enough to engage the public with the message that prison is costly, counter-productive and, except in a very few cases, in no one's interests. This may seem like a pipedream, but there are various signs that this can be achieved.

There have been a number of pro-abolition initiatives recently, including one in which I played a small part, Esme Fairbairn's Rethinking Crime and Punishment initiative (for more information on this see www.rethinking.org.uk). The Howard League for Penal Reform (www.howardleague.org/), for whom I act as Vice Chairman, also continues its long record of campaigning for prison form, and conducted a vigorous campaign against prisons at the last General Election, part of a wider attempt to raise the level of debate about crime and punishment. This had various politicians on the back foot and resulted in Millbank having to guide their candidates in what to say if they were challenged about prisons on the doorstep. Inevitably, this Millbank advice was almost immediately leaked to The Howard League!

However, perhaps we could see such initiatives as part of the traditional response to imprisonment and prisons. In their different ways these make a contribution to the 'mood music' and to policy - some to a greater extent than others - but, for different reasons, they still fall short of creating the space in which a challenge to prison can be mounted. I say this because I think that

*Prisons and how to get rid of them*

there was a wider space for scepticism about prisons at the time of our historical example than there is today. We thus have to work to create what Mathiesen describes in his book as an 'alternative public space'.

One way to do this is through an engagement with the media. For example the Channel 4 series *Buried* (for which I acted as a consultant) generated more column inches about penal reform - and at a stroke a bigger potential constituency in support of penal reform - than any other event of the last five years.[5] *Buried* (no matter what you might think of it as drama, and I am aware of several recent criticisms of the programme from penal insiders such as Jamie Bennett) exposed the still largely closed world of prison to public scrutiny, and presented for all to see the violence, hopelessness, madness and pervading sense of decay that permeates prison. It is a tragedy that *Buried* did not get commissioned for another series, in spite of its popularity. Nonetheless, there will be other *Burieds*, and we should do what we can to support the space that programmes like this create. It is in spaces like this that a challenge to imprisonment can take hold, with an audience that does not normally think too much about prison or prisoners. *Buried* helped to create such a space because it seemed 'real'; it seemed genuine, unlike the obvious fakery of *Porridge*. The series appealed to people's emotions, and allowed them to engage at a personal level with the lives of prisoners and their families and friends.

The reaction to *Buried* influenced my approach in writing my book *Death at the Hands of the State* (see note 2). I gave a lot of thought to the question of how to engage an audience with a reductionist/abolitionist agenda. I didn't want to reproduce the same old mountain of evidence about the irrationality of prison, simply for that evidence to yet again be ignored. How could an audience for penal abolition be created? As I have indicated, what struck me about *Buried* was the power of its emotional appeal to the audience. It told believable stories about believable people - prisoners - who were just like you and me, and who were worried about the same things that you and I worry about: families, relationships, finding work, surviving, consuming, and simply progressing through life. So, in my book I decided to tell stories - emotional stories - and to infuse the argument with a narrative based on real people who ended up inside, or who had family

---

5. I have written elsewhere about cinema's use of prisons and imprisonment; see my *Images of Incarceration* (co-authored with Sean O'Sullivan), Waterside Press 2004.

members who had ended up inside. I also told stories about the scandal of the numbers of people who die whilst in our penal system, especially children.

I decided to tell stories about people like Pauline Campbell - a modern-day suffragette. Pauline is a former college lecturer in her late 50s, who during 2004 was arrested more than ten times as a direct result of her own unique protest, which is aimed at drawing attention to the deaths of women prisoners in British jails. Every time a woman died, Campbell would go to the prison where the death had occurred and stand in the road, to prevent prison vans from bringing more women to that jail. The police would be called and Campbell would then be ordered by them to move out of the van's way. She'd refuse and then she'd be arrested. She describes this as her 'one woman, self-funding protest'.

Campbell began this protest campaign after the death of her only child Sarah, who died at the age of 18 in January 2003, whilst in the 'so-called care of HMP & YOI Styal'. Sarah had spent six months on remand in 2002 and on 17 January 2003 was sentenced to a term of imprisonment and returned to Styal. The following day Sarah was taken unconscious to a local hospital, where she died later that evening without regaining consciousness. Campbell says that she protests to 'demonstrate that prisons are unsafe places which constantly failed to uphold the duty of care that the Prison Service has to all prisoners'. She describes the service as medieval and feels impelled to speak out against it. She held her first demonstration outside HMP Brockhill, following the death of Sheena Kotecha, her second outside HMP Holloway when Julie Hope died, and a third outside HMP New Hall after the death of Louise Davis. Since then the demonstrations have carried on, for women in prison are forty times more likely to kill themselves than women in the community as a whole.[6] Indeed in 2004 12 women - a new record - took their lives in English and Welsh jails and so, tragically, Campbell is rarely out of the news.

I use Pauline Campbell's emotional story - and many other stories about people like her in the book - to shamelessly connect the audience with the scandal of what happens behind our prison's walls. In doing so I do not pretend to be objective, empirical or indeed logical. Rather I am emotional, partisan and passionate, and through that passion I hope to engage the reader with the cause

---

6. D. Rickford, *Troubled Inside: Responding to the Mental Health Needs of Women in Prison*, PRT 2003.

of prison contraction and abolition. After all, prison and penal expansionists have been adept at using logic and objectivity to mask their policy goals; I felt that such canons of the academic culture were perhaps not the best means for making the abolitionist case, in a context in which the contours of alternative public space are still being shaped and defined. In short, what I wanted to do was create a scandal: when we start to think of the things that happen behind the walls of our prisons as scandalous, I know we will have begun to travel on the road towards decarceration.

Having said all of this, I want to end with a plea and a challenge to readers of this article - who no doubt include academics, policy-makers, *Guardian* readers, and others who may have no knowledge of prisons. The alternative space that needs to be created has also to be created by you. You are not passive within that space, but rather can have a key role in resisting the mass incarceration that is currently taking place in this country. After all, you are 'real' in this debate too. But, aside from a few notable exceptions, where has been your voice? Where has been your opposition? Can you really stay silent about the scandal that goes on behind prison walls, as more and more people are sent inside, for having committed fewer and less severe offences? We must all be prepared to challenge the hyper-incarceration of this country, but a challenge cannot be made by keeping silent, nor the truth revealed by keeping quiet. So make some noise, and create some scandal, or watch as our prison numbers grow and grow, again and again.

Soundings, Issue 33, Summer 2006

# The Mothers of May Square

## Richard Minns

*Richard Minns describes a unique political movement.*

Thirty thousand (mainly young) people 'disappeared' during the 1976-83 junta in Argentina. Many were tortured, drugged, and thrown out of helicopters over the River Plate. The most consistent and unquenchable protest against this disappearance of the young has been from the Mothers of May Square, an organisation formed on 30 April 1977, one year after the military coup. Now elderly, these women continue to organise, but no longer for their lost children. They have become energetic and respected campaigners for human rights, defying the allotted role for women as the despairing mourners of society.

Hebe de Bonafini is the President of the Mothers of May Square. Her office is adorned with photos and posters of Che Guevara and Fidel Castro. The sign on her kitchen door proclaims 'welcome comandantes', with two faces wearing baraclavas. The office serves as the HQ of the movement, and also as a congenial cafe/bistro, with home-made food, and a radical bookshop. If you want to buy books about the revolutionary history of South America, the CIA-inspired death of Salvador Allende in Chile (the other 9/11), the history and murder of Che Guevara, the struggle of the indigenous people of Peru, Brazil, and Colombia, this is the place. Photos show her with the zapatistas in the Chiapas, with subcomandante Marcos, and in Palestine with the late President Yasser Arafat, in Iraq, Italy, Austria, France, Netherlands, Canada, Philippines, Germany, in London working for the extradition of General Pinochet of Chile, and paying tribute at memorials to twentieth-century atrocities and struggles across the world, for example the Warsaw ghetto and uprising. She has been physically

The Mothers of May Square

attacked, arrested and detained.

Hebe de Bonafini is one of the most polite and articulate people involved in the pursuit of justice and rights. But the movement has changed according to the circumstances of the last thirty years, and it has split because of the differing, tragic histories of the young people and children involved in 'el processo' (the dictatorship).

I was awed by the deference accorded her, first by my interpreter) and then by my photographer. But Hebe de Bonafini is not surprised by anything. Books about the history of 'the Mothers' show photographs of her with the Pope (ironically, given the church's complicity in promoting Nazism in Argentina), leaders of the western and south American world, with actresses and campaigners such as Liv Ullman and Vanessa Redgrave, as well as musicians such as Sting and U2 (who visited the bookshop/HQ in 1998).

For years, the Mothers were accorded some respect simply because they were bereaved mothers. But what have they actually achieved, and what have been the difficulties? The answer is that the movement has had to change. Initially they pursued the military who were culpable. After the fall of the junta, when the military were granted exemption from prosecution and trial by President Raul

Pic 1: Hebe de Bonafini

Alfonsin, the Mothers campaigned continuously against the government. They finally achieved some success in this, with the lifting of the embargo on prosecution of former alleged culprits by the Argentine Supreme Court in June 2005.

In the meantime, however, their whole philosophy has been transformed. They gave up the pursuit of the military as their main objective ten years ago, on the grounds that their children will never be found, and that 'we are the Mothers of every lost child'. They feel that the bodies and spirits of their lost children live on in the young people of today. Looking for dead bodies is futile, and the military will always escape. Therefore they have argued that they must become a movement for human rights, and stop thinking about the dead, who have gone. 'The white headscarf must not be identified with death', they proclaim, and no Mother wears the name of her dead child on her headscarf.

They reject the idea of compensation for their dead children (although some have split off from the movement and accepted some financial reparation). In doing so they have raised fundamental questions about what to do in horrific circumstances such as these.

Part of their approach has been to form a university (opened in April 2000) for poor people, the unemployed and the 'piqueteros' (pickets) campaigning against

*Pic 2 below: Casa de las Madres, Pic 3 opposite: Poster for the Popular University*

AL
de febrer
Seman
Cortáza
LITERATURA - CINE
PSICODRAMA - POLITIC
MUSICA - DEBATES
Y la voz de Julio Cortáz
Universidad Popular
Madres de Plaza de Mayo
ENTRAD
LIBRE

closed factories and unemployment. A rock concert was held to raise money. Scholarships are awarded to piqueteros and street gleaners (cartoneros) who trawl the streets each night for rubbish and cardboard that can be recycled. Professional teachers from other universities give up their time to teach there for nothing.

'From death, and the past, to life and the future', as Hebe de Bonafini would say. Their courses include social psychology, cinema, human rights, cooperative organisation, political and social economy, and drama. Short courses include seminars on Marx's *Capital*, social conflict at work, and the history of Latin America and Argentina. Pupils are admitted who do not have the requisite qualifications for conventional universities. By the start of 2005, they had 1400 students and 100 part-time teachers.

The political strategy has changed too. Instead of criticising everything the government does, they now accept compromises, although they refuse public subsidy for the university, alongside the policy of no money for reparations for their dead children.

The interesting point is the way this movement has changed in accordance with the difficulties which have arisen in dire circumstances. There are lessons here for all social movements.

*Pic 4: Poster showing some of the disappeared*

Part of the revised philosophy about the dead and young people has been their decision to help in the case against politicians and others implicated in the fire in the Cromagnon disco/rock club in December 2004. No less than 193 young people died in the fire, after all the doors and emergency exits had been locked to stop gatecrashers. The shoes of the dead are suspended from telegraph wires and cables outside the club, across the street in the aptly named Plaza Miserere; others are accumulated in a pile alongside photos and dedications to the dead - an emotive display.

Their new politics is 'to try and change the attitude of the world'. Hebe de Bonafini certainly gets around that world. And when you see elderly women - wearing their white headscarves - returning to the cafe from their Thursday afternoon stint in May Square, and you take note of their extensive international contacts and campaigns, you believe it may be possible.

The change in philosophy or objectives has been vital. The Mothers influence governments and international relations in Argentina. This is 'grey power' at its ultimate. Nothing to do with old-age pensions and retirement benefits (my favourite subject): just human rights and how to fight for them in extreme circumstances, translating an intractable endeavour into a practical project.

And it remains totally a women's movement - declining in numbers of course as the elderly women die - led by a person who should be nominated for a Nobel peace prize (although, knowing her character slightly, she would probably refuse it).

*All photos © Eliana Moscovich*

*The Madres de Plaza de Mayo can be contacted at the people's university - universidad@madres.org; www.madres.org (Universidad Popular, Madres de Plaza de Mayo - universidad de lucha y resistencia, Hipólito Irigoyen 1584, Buenos Aires, Argentina).*

*Soundings*, Issue 33, Summer 2006

# Westward look, the land is bright

## Race and politics in the Andes

### Richard Gott

*Richard Gott discusses the emergence of important new political players in Latin America, often based on new alliances between the armed forces and indigenous movements.*

Something new and interesting, and profoundly original, has been taking place in Latin America in the early years of this century, deserving close attention from all those left depressed or made cynical by global developments in the years since 1989. Seismic political upheavals have occurred in countries that once seemed permanently lulled to sleep by the siren voices of neo-liberalism, encapsulated within the so-called Washington Consensus'.

This US-inspired project, first codified in 1989, sought to reform the economic programmes of Latin American governments through a radical reduction in public spending, the privatisation of state enterprises, the encouragement of foreign investment, and the liberalisation of trade and finance. Part of the neo-liberal counter-revolution, and overseen by the International Monetary Fund and the World Bank, it promised huge improvements in economic performance, and was widely welcomed as though there were no alternative.

Yet in practice its imposition led to vastly increased unemployment and to the further impoverishment of huge swathes of the population. The eventual rebellions against these programmes have seen the emergence of important new political players, some drawn from the armed forces, others from Latin America's indigenous movements. An entirely fresh and radical spirit is abroad, bringing the question of race and ethnic difference to the surface, not as a simple petition for indigenous 'rights' but as a demand for a restructuring of the old colonial, white settler state. This has the flavour of a genuine revolution.

In the countries of the Andes in particular - Bolivia, Peru and Ecuador - the rebellious movements created by the indigenous peoples, the majority of the population, have begun for the first time to make a major impact, introducing a new and transforming element into the politics of the region. Indeed the cultural resurgence of groups reclaiming their indigenous identity can be detected throughout the continent - from Argentina to Venezuela, from Chile to Brazil, from Colombia to Mexico. The ruling elite in countries like Chile and Argentina, traditionally imagining their country to be as white as Australia, have been shocked to find themselves sharing their territorial space with people who claim an aboriginal background.

The appearance of these indigenous movements has appeared in the foreign media with little explanation or analysis. Yet they represent a sea-change in the politics of Latin America. The indigenous peoples, heirs to the age-old civilisations of the continent, have been stirring themselves politically for the first time since the eighteenth century. Now highly politicised, they have grown strong enough to overthrow governments.

The continuing displacement of native peoples from the countryside, accelerated during the neo-liberal years, has produced immense new indigenous cities, often invisible to the white middle class. These rural refugees have been driven from their homes by the collapse of the tin mines, by oil prospectors, by logging companies, and by coca eradication programmes. Lima in the coastal plain of Peru has become a Quechua city, peopled by the inhabitants of the high plateau; the Chilean capital, Santiago, is now surrounded by shanty towns of Mapuches, the indigenous peoples driven out of their forest reservations in the south; the Ecuadorean capital of Quito has doubled in size in recent years; while El Alto, the new Aymara city on the high Bolivian plateau, often threatens to overwhelm La Paz, the capital in the valley below.

The population of these new urban conglomerations, thanks to modern methods of communication, often retain their rural culture and remain in constant touch with their rural roots. They also make fresh connections with their ethnic counterparts in the countries next door. Their cities have become a political tinder-box, inexorably changing the balance of power throughout the Andes.

The new movements of indigenous peoples have been causing considerable alarm within the local conservative (and racist) political establishments, as well as in the United States. A recent headline in a Miami newspaper read: 'War on Terror has Latin America's Indigenous People in its Sights'. Some academics argue that the growth of the indigenous movements is merely an extension of the democratic practice developed in the continent since the defeat of the dictatorships. Latin America once extended the franchise to the working class, so why should it not now incorporate the indigenous peoples? In theory that sounds plausible, yet Latin America's ruling elite has been notably reluctant to embrace this new democracy. The reason lies in its racist fear, deeply etched over the centuries, of the gigantic underclass with which it shares the continent.

Debates within the continent's once powerful leftist movements have also been affected by the indigenous upsurge. Gender issues and liberation theology were taken on board in the last decades of the twentieth century, but many on the left have been unprepared to deal with questions associated with culture, race, and popular religion. For in parallel with the growth of indigenous politics has come an explosion of evangelical chapels, threatening the ancient monopoly of the Catholic Church. These developments have been greeted with confusion or rejection by the left. Little guidance on all this can be found in the classical texts.

Some of the indigenous peoples of the Andes have been making unprecedented and utopian demands. Bolivian radicals have been calling for the revival of the Aymara nation in the Altiplano that preceded the arrival of the Spanish conquistadors. Peruvians have talked about the return of Tahuantinsuyo - the 'four states' of the old Inca empire of 500 years ago that stretched from Pasto in Colombia to the River Maule in Chile, and over the Andes to Tucumán in Argentina.

Such developments are not peculiar to Latin America. They have elements in common with comparable phenomena in other parts of the world. The revival of local and indigenous cultures across borders, and the desire to redraw the artificial frontiers established in colonial times, is a familiar theme in contemporary Africa. The United States itself has seen a significant revival of indigenous activity - with the revived memory of old battles and the reclaiming of ancient land rights. Yet the experience of Latin America, different though in some ways similar to what has been happening elsewhere, has rarely been bracketed together in a common analysis.

In their early years, in the 1990s, the new indigenous movements received a certain amount of assistance from outside - chiefly through example. The upsurge of indigenous activism in the United States preceded that in Latin America, and US activists were already making visits to the southern continent in the 1980s. The movements in Latin American took off seriously after 1992, when official festivities were held to record the 500th anniversary of the Columbus landings. These became a celebration of the continuing survival of the indigenous nations rather than of the achievements of the white settler societies. A UN declaration describing the 1990s as 'the decade of indigenous peoples' also gave a focus to the new movements.

An antiquarian strand, sometimes called *indigenismo*, has long permeated Latin American thinking about the pre-Colombian peoples. Whites in Cuba in the nineteenth century wrote novels about the island's heroic indigenous past, the phenomenon known as *siboneyismo*. In Peru in the 1920s Juan Carlos Mariátegui, an early Marxist, invoked the country's Inca heritage and called for the Andean peoples to be integrated into the nation. But the developments of the 1990s are new and different in that demands are being made by the indigenous people themselves - through increasingly vocal and well-organised political organisations.

The indigenous movements are not alone. Other forces are at work in the current upsurge in radical protest. In the southern cone countries of Argentina and Uruguay, a revival of the progressive tempo of the early 1970s has begun to surface, an apparent generational throwback to earlier experiments cut short by the military interventions of that sinister decade. The heirs of the radical Young Peronists (in Argentina) and the Tupamaros guerrillas (in Uruguay) are now in power through popular election. Social movements that had mobilised around the concept of 'civil society', abandoning the prospect of securing political power at the centre, suddenly found that this unexpected possibility had become a reality. Not least among the intriguing developments of the new millennium has been the surprising capacity of popular movements to use the ballot box as a source of unity rather than division, producing election results often undetected by opinion polls.

One remarkable phenomenon has been the comeback of Cuba and its formidable leader Fidel Castro, now in his eightieth year and enjoying a position of respect throughout the continent. Banished from inter-American councils since 1961 by US diktat, and suffering from nearly half a century of economic sanctions unilaterally imposed by the United States, Cuba has re-established diplomatic and business links with most of the continent, bringing increased trade and finance as well as fresh and much-needed intellectual contacts to this too long isolated island.

Castro himself, largely ignored or derided in Europe as an authoritarian dictator, is now perceived throughout Latin America as a wise and benign elder statesman, one of the great figures of the twentieth century, in the pantheon with Nelson Mandela. Sought after by students and journalists wherever he goes, he is also waylaid by Presidents anxious for a photo-opportunity or simply for a word of approval. Cuba's success in resisting US pressure over such a long period is displayed as a badge of honour, recognised as such in the current climate of overt anti-imperialism - itself the result of the foreign policy of the US administration of George W Bush, unpopular throughout the continent among all groups.

A mood of expectant optimism now prevails in much of Latin America, a welcome change after three decades of political inertia. For years the adherents to the Washington Consensus were able to rule with barely a squawk of protest from within the political system (though with considerable popular upheaval taking place outside). The astonishing victory of Evo Morales, a radical indigenous leader, in the presidential elections in Bolivia of December 2006, has served to focus attention on a widely touted 'move to the left' that has characterised the early years of the new millennium. Foreign journalists and television crews have been trying to catch up after years of ignorance and neglect.

The language of Evo Morales, never less than direct, gives the flavour of the new era. 'This is a confrontation between rich and poor', he told an interviewer in his office in the Congress building in March 2005, 'but it's also a racial conflict'.

'Look at them', he said, pointing to photographs of former congressmen over the past hundred years. 'Almost all those people are white. They hate the fact that I'm an Indian. They hate that we're here.'

He was speaking under a poster of his smiling face with the legend: 'While the poor have no bread, the rich will have no peace.' Fighting talk. 'They have humiliated and looted for hundreds of years', Morales told the journalist. 'We are trying to put a stop to that now.'

This is the uncompromising voice of Latin America's indigenous peoples now making itself heard. Morales is the latest example of the radical mood in the continent, but the new political era began some years ago with the election of Hugo Chávez as President in Venezuela in December 1998. A charismatic former army officer with an overtly revolutionary programme (which included an entire chapter of a new constitution devoted to indigenous peoples), Chávez has begun talking recently about the need to formulate a 'socialism for the twenty-first century'. His victory was followed by that of Lula de Silva in Brazil in 2002, Nestor Kirchner in Argentina in 2003, Tabaré Vásquez in Uruguay in 2005, Evo Morales in Bolivia, and Michelle Bachelet in Chile in 2006.

Following down the pipeline this year has come Ollanta Humala in Peru, a left-wing former officer who, though he did not in the end win, drew on massive indigenous support in the presidential elections in June. In Mexico Andrés Manuel López Obregón, a former radical mayor of Mexico City, is a strong presidential candidate; in September there are good prospects for the elections in Ecuador (where a possible candidate is Rafael Correa, a radical economist); and Daniel Ortega, the former Sandinista leader, will probably win the elections in Nicaragua in November. All come from ideological strands in the Latin American spectrum that are recognisably to the left.

Clearly this is not a homogenous left; their programmes and political processes are specific to each country. Some have an outspoken rhetoric hostile to neo-liberalism, others are happy with the way things are. Yet they do have several things in common. All share a strong sense of nationalism, the revival of a historic Latin American characteristic that has been strikingly dormant in the neo-liberal years. All are critical of the excessive US cultural influence in the continent, as well as its more familiar political presence; and all (with the exception of Chile) have indicated their hostility to the US project of creating a Latin American Free Trade Area, and share a vision of an integrated Latin America free from its

Soundings

northern overlord.

These are small acorns, yet the outlines of a common agenda can be mistily discerned. While the word 'socialism' is used sparingly, many of these new leftist governments are also beginning to foresee a new role for the state. There is no intention to return to the large-scale nationalisations that characterised, say, the Chilean government of Salvador Allende in the 1970s. Yet many now see the need for the state to control, or more closely to oversee, their countries' extractive industries. The recovery of governmental control over the nationalised oil industry of Venezuela by Hugo Chávez, securing increased revenues from royalties and taxes, is widely seen as a model. What has worked in Venezuela is being copied in Bolivia, and Evo Morales announced on May Day 2006 that foreign companies would have six months to renegotiate their contracts. They would be expected to cede to the state their existing ownership rights to energy resources, and to pay higher royalties and taxes. The companies have made appropriate noises of discomfort, yet with the continuing high price of oil they will have little cause for complaint. If radical governments emerge in Peru and Ecuador, the same recipe will be tried.

Also significant in many of countries with left-leaning governments is the presence of mobilised social movements operating in the background. These have been working for the most part as independent actors, yet they have proved capable of dramatic political intervention, and include the *Movimento Sem Terra* (MST) in Brazil (the Movement of Landless Workers), and the *piqueteros*, or 'strikers', in Argentina. This movement developed from the actions of unemployed workers in northern Argentina, thrown out of work by the privatisations of the 1980s and 1990s. Spreading widely throughout the country, the *piqueteros* brought Buenos Aires to a standstill in December 2001, provoking a prolonged political crisis of which Nestor Kirchner was the eventual beneficiary. Together with the indigenous movements in Bolivia and CONAIE in Ecuador (the *Confederación de Nacionalidades Indígenas*), these have all become permanent features of the political scene, unimaginable in the years of military dictatorship.

## The revolt against the Washington consensus

The move to the left is largely the outcome of the economic and political failure of the Washington Consensus. This formidable, counter-revolutionary neo-liberal project, first imposed in Chile in the mid-1970s, spread throughout the continent in the two subsequent decades. The Chilean programmes were originally elaborated by General Pinochet's 'Chicago Boys', eager monetarists schooled at the University of Chicago, who began their work in 1975. The privatisation of state industries took off after 1978, and the Chilean model was finally established in the 1980s, combining free markets with a repressive political system. It was much admired by the new conservative governments of Eastern Europe (and China) after 1989.

Bolivia was next in line to imbibe the neo-liberal medicine. In 1986 it fell into the hands of Jeffrey Sachs, a then youthful Harvard economic guru who went on later to help dismantle the statist economies of Eastern Europe. (He subsequently repented somewhat to become the director of the Earth Institute at Columbia University.) One result of Sachs's recommendations to the Bolivian government was an end to the scourge of hyper-inflation that had affected the economy in the 1980s. Less welcome was the advice to halt the government subsidy to the country's historic tin mines, a decision that led inevitably to their economic collapse and closure, throwing thousands of miners out of work.

After Bolivia came Venezuela, where an arrogant attempt in 1989 to drive through an emergency neo-liberal programme (put forward, as in Bolivia and Chile, by clever young US-educated economists) was greeted with street protests in Caracas on an unprecedented scale. The so-called *Caracazo* of February 1989 marked the start of the fight-back in Latin America against the neo-liberal order. The protests were perceived as regime-threatening, the army was called in to crush them, and more than a thousand people were killed. A further decade of economic and political deterioration (involving two attempted military coups, the successful impeachment of the President, and the collapse of the country's principal bank) led to the implosion of the corrupt old political system and the eventual emergence at the end of the 1990s of Colonel Chávez.

'while there is no intention to return to large-scale nationalisations, many of these new leftist governments are beginning to see a new role for the state'

After Venezuela came Ecuador, where a political explosion in 1990 marked the formal start of the new politics in the Andes: the emergence of indigenous movements demanding their political rights. That year a hundred indigenous activists occupied the cathedral in Quito, to demand action from the government

113

to resolve a land dispute in the Sierra. Later in 1990 the unrest spread to Bolivia where indigenous groups from the lowlands of the Beni began a long protest march to La Paz, their anger provoked by another neo-liberal phenomenon: the arrival of foreign logging companies moving onto their land.

The demonstration in Quito sparked an insurrection throughout the highlands, and the government was obliged to recognise CONAIE as the legitimate voice of the Indian majority. CONAIE had been established a few years earlier, in 1986, by Ecuador's 11 principal indigenous nations.

Land conflicts and the increasing politicisation of the indigenous movements led to the creation of Ecuador's first indigenous political party in 1995. Pachakutik, or the Movement of Pluri-national Unity, developed a radical rhetoric that went far beyond a demand for the recognition of land rights. The initial three slogans of the movement were 'no corruption, no lies, no idleness' [*'ama sua, ama llulla, ama kjella'*], but eventually it came out with more specific complaints against the Quito government's neo-liberal programme, moving into top gear when the government, with IMF advice, adopted the US dollar as the national currency.

In January 2000 a rebellion was ignited by Pachakutik supporters, backed by young army officers. They seized the Congress building in Quito and brought down the government. Colonel Luis Gutiérrez, one of the young officers, was elected President three years later with the support of Pachakutik. This first experiment in the Andes of an alliance between the military and the indigenous movements lasted for less than a year, for Colonel Gutiérrez refused to abandon the neo-liberal policies of his predecessors. He retained the US dollar, and Pachakutik withdrew its support. A further rebellion in 2005 led to his overthrow and replacement by an interim President, Alfredo Palacios.

Meanwhile something similar was taking place in Bolivia, where the indigenous movements had also organised a Pachakutik movement in the 1990s, with the same three demands as the movement in Ecuador - no corruption, no lies, no idleness. Felipe Quispe, their leader among the Aymara, talked of the communal Eden that had existed before the Spanish conquest, and, like the indigenous leaders in Ecuador, he often used the anti-capitalist language of the anti-globalisation movements. He called for capitalism to be replaced by an economic system based on the three ancient pillars of pre-Colombian society, and for the country's artificial borders to be redrawn. Quispe was soon overtaken in political realism and in popularity by Evo Morales, another Aymara leader, who

*Westward look, the land is bright*

allied himself to politicians outside the indigenous movement, notably Alvaro García Linera (who would become his Vice-President). Their political group, the Movement to Socialism, secured support beyond the indigenous population in the *mestizo* middle class and in the relics of the old trade union movement.

As a result of the drastic closure of the tin mines in the 1980s, the class-conscious and highly unionised mining workforce, now without work, had been translated from the cold plateau of the Altiplano to the semi-tropical coca fields of the Chapare. There these former miners cultivated coca, the most profitable work available. Their unscheduled move had an unexpected impact on the country's politics, for their old union activism, deployed in this fresh setting, was soon to join with that of the emerging indigenous movements to create a successful electoral tide.

At presidential elections in June 2002, Morales came a close second to Sánchez de Losada, a right-wing millionaire with close links to the American embassy. A year later, in October 2003, La Paz was given over to demonstrators protesting against his privatisation programme. The indigenous population streamed down from the hills to attack US fast-food outlets and supermarkets, and Sánchez de Losada fled into exile in the United States, to be replaced by his deputy, Carlos Mesa.

The popular protest bubbling away in the Andes had a particular focus on the various neo-liberal attempts to privatise the municipal water supply, a project that proved particularly offensive to indigenous opinion. Demonstrations in Cochabamba in April 2000 led to the cancellation of a water contract with the US firm Bechtel, and similar protests in El Alto in January 2005 led to the withdrawal of a French water firm, Lyonnaise des Eaux, which had been operating there since 1997.

Protests in Bolivia against water privatisation were soon extended to the government's apparent 'give away' of the country's oil and natural gas reserves, and these led in June 2005 to the resignation of President Mesa and to the eventual electoral victory of Evo Morales in December.

A similar story has been unfolding in Peru, hitherto less exposed to indigenous politics than the other Andean countries. The terrible cost of the repression of *Sendero Luminoso*, the Maoist guerrilla movement of the 1980s, which led to more than 70,000 deaths, left people with little appetite for politics. Yet in the year 2000 a coalition similar to that in Ecuador, of military officers and indigenous organisations, supported a rebellion by two young officers, Ollanta and Antauro Humala. Their rebellion accelerated the downfall of the neo-liberal government of Alberto Fujimori, and in subsequent years, the Humala brothers created a countrywide organisation with an indigenous and nationalist agenda that sought to resurrect the government and geographical space of the Inca empire.

Their movement's magazine, *Ollanta*, selling more than 60,000 copies each fortnight, campaigned against privatisation, globalisation and the free-market system adopted by successive Peruvian governments. *Ollanta*'s message went down well in a country where more than half the population is Quechua or Aymara. Peruvian social movements were closely watching events in Bolivia and demonstrations in Arequipa in 2002 halted the sale of local water companies to a Belgian firm.

Antauro Humala organised a fresh rebellion in January 2005, seizing the Andean town of Andahuaylas with a group of 200 former soldiers. Their call for the resignation of President Alejandro Toledo secured the support of thousands of local people, who came out on the streets to express their solidarity. Government forces soon regained control of the town, but the explosive potential of the Andean highlands stood revealed.

Ollanta Humala became the frontrunner in this year's presidential campaign, distancing himself from his brother's version of what has become known as 'ethno-nationalism' on the grounds that it was too right-wing. Ollanta prefers the left-wing language of Hugo Chávez.

Latin America's white elite has been virulently hostile to the emergence of the indigenous movements in the Andes. In Peru, Mario Vargas Llosa, the novelist and former right-wing presidential candidate (now a Spanish citizen), is an outspoken critic, accusing them of generating 'political and social disorder'. Society faces a choice, he says, between civilisation and barbarism. This is the age-old cry of Latin America's white settlers, an indication of their unwillingness to come to terms with the indigenous peoples whose continent they have usurped.

Similar sentiments have been expressed by the opposition in Venezuela, where the pronounced hostility to Chávez from the old ruling elite comes more from race hatred than from class prejudice. Chávez has not hurt the rich in their pocket, only in their *amour propre*. By addressing the neglected question of the black and indigenous majority of the population, he has reminded the rich whites of the real nature of the society in which they live.

The prevalence of the free market, once thought to presage 'the end of history', has certainly thrown up some intriguing new actors on the political stage, although maybe it is too early to map out their ultimate impact. The indigenous movements are by no means homogenous and have a disconcerting tendency to quarrel and divide. Each ethnic group has its own traditions and its own leader, and unites with others with difficulty.

Yet their presence at the political centre is now well-established. Their flamboyant eruption signposts the creation and growth of a cultural resistance to the globalising trends that have swept the world in the years since the collapse of communism. As well as bringing increased poverty to the already poor, the onslaught of economic neo-liberalism was also accompanied by a cultural invasion that has affected the development of individual countries in important ways: the import of American-style consumer habits has influenced what people grow and what they eat, where they shop and what they wear, and what they watch at the cinema and on television.

Globalisation had also brought a particular form of liberal democracy, often at odds with local tradition. Old political parties have been undermined and cast aside, while new forms of political campaigning have arrived as part of a package 'Made-in-the-USA'. Huge sums have been spent on election advertising, particularly on television, and on the commissioning of marketing and opinion polls. Freshly revived concepts have been encouraged, like 'civil society' and 'human rights', that have little echo in Latin America's traditional political vocabulary.

While the new cult of globalisation has been accepted by Latin America's dominant elites, their position is increasingly insecure. They remain delicately balanced above a seething mass of discontented humanity. The problem for the globalisers is that Latin America is composed of many countries with little cultural or social homogeneity. The white settler elites may welcome the culture and practice that comes from another settler society, but these are anathema to the indigenous inhabitants, at war with the settlers for five centuries.

In breaking away from the political parties of the white settlers, and in giving their support to their own emerging movements, the indigenous peoples are promoting and sustaining the growth of a new cultural nationalism that is beginning to erode the forces of globalisation.

Three countries so far have embraced the cause of cultural nationalism at the level of the state - Castro's Cuba, Chávez's Venezuela, and Morales's Bolivia. All have supported the struggle of the indigenous peoples, and all have emphasised their own history of liberation struggle going back over the centuries. All have sought to give value and respect to their traditional underclass, and to use their sense of history as a weapon to defeat the globalisers.

In doing so they have revived an argument in Latin America that goes back at least as far as Simón Bolívar and José Martí. 'Our history is different from that of the United States or Europe', they argue. 'Our culture is different, our politics are different, and so too is our economic system. And our countries have a right to define what our future will be, without being told what to do by the World Bank, the International Monetary Fund, or the World Trade Organisation.' Maybe such ideas may be seen eventually as a force for change, and not just in Latin America.

# Eurasia at the crossroads

## Christoph Bluth

*Christoph Bluth looks at the challenges and opportunities facing the countries of Central Asia.*

The international system at the beginning of the twenty-first century has been characterised by the simultaneous processes of globalisation and regionalisation; by the shift from global power politics to geo-economics; the decline of Great Power rivalry; and the emergence of regional conflicts and international terrorism. Within this context, much attention has been focused on the countries at the southern periphery of the former Soviet Union. These lie in the strategic juncture between two major powers with nuclear arsenals, Russia and China, and at the interface between Russia and the Islamic world. This position, and their rich natural resources, as exemplified in the energy resources of the Caspian region, define the strategic environment for these new states and their population of over 55 million people.

The war on terror, and particularly the war in Afghanistan, has fundamentally affected the Eurasian region.[1] But there are many other factors that have an impact on peace and stability there. Lack of economic development, wealth inequality and the level of poverty are the principal threats to state security in the region; and these all contribute to the potential for ethnic and regional conflict. The possession by the states of Central Asia of significant mineral wealth is also a crucial factor in the region: the potential contribution of energy and other natural resources to economic development is fundamental to public policy and the interests of the states. The geopolitical context is that Eurasia

1. Eurasia is used here in the sense that it has acquired of referring to the now independent Central Asian states that were once part of the Soviet Union.

was in Russia's sphere of influence for a very long time, but its influence, though still considerable, is now more subject to contestation; the region has recently been affected by the removal of the Taliban regime in Afghanistan, the shift of terrorism to the centre of the international security agenda and the direct involvement of the United States in the region.

The involvement of outside powers - including the United States, the European Union, China and Turkey - and their willingness to contribute to security is influenced by the prospects for the development of energy resources: the transport of energy demands the removal of threats to security (including terrorism). And in as much as energy can provide economic stability, this should in itself help to provide security to the region.

The international system in the southern region of the former Soviet Union is now in flux and is being shaped by a number of factors. Firstly, international terrorism is now at the centre of the international security agenda. The involvement of major powers, especially the United States, in the region is therefore likely for the foreseeable future. States are competing for US military and financial support. The war on terrorism also has a substantial and lasting impact on the energy industry, and the energy resources of the Caspian region in particular. A second process of change is Russia's role within the region. Russia formerly considered Central Asia to be in its sphere of national interest. This policy was directed at preserving Russian interests, including border security, protecting the interests of ethnic Russians and economic assets (including control over energy resources), and keeping out potential rivals such as China, Turkey, Iran or the United States. This policy has not been abandoned, but the US presence in the region marks a shift that could presage a more significant long-range geopolitical change.

In spite of such developments on the international front, however, the main threat to regional stability is internal - economic and political. On the economic front, the lack of economic development is significant, as is the economic downturn since the dissolution of the Soviet Union and the resulting social problems. On the political front, there are immense internal ethnic and political tensions in these states, whose identities and institutions have not found new forms since the Soviet collapse In the late 1990s religious extremism came to be perceived as a serious threat to the stability of Central Asian states. In 1999 a number of bombs exploded in Tashkent in a determined, albeit failed, attempt to kill President Karimov. Since 1999 the Islamic Movement of Uzbekistan has periodically engaged in terrorist activities in the Ferghana valley, a region that has been a focus of conflict between Uzbekistan, Tajikistan and the Kyrgyz Republic. This conflict has its roots in the civil conflict in Tajikistan, disputes over water resources, and the drug traffic from Afghanistan into the other Newly Independent States. The failure of the Caspian governments to effectively promote economic and political development and prevent substantial economic and social dislocation needs to be addressed if the influence of extremist Islamic groups is to be mitigated.

Economic performance and governmental economic policies are going to be crucially important for the Caspian Sea region in the next period. Economic growth (insofar as it is based on the development of mineral resources) will not in itself guarantee better living standards, a greater number of choices, or a more secure existence for the majority of the population. But it is nevertheless a necessary pre-condition for the development of all these. The principal question for the governments in this region is whether or not they will have the ability, vision and willingness to make good use of their rich mineral resources. In the case of Caspian Sea region, policy is constrained by the need to retain public confidence in the context of limited financial resources.

Poverty and inequality are multidimensional phenomena, which affect all Eurasian economies. The substantial deterioration of the economic situation after 1992 was accompanied by systematic asset-stripping by the political elites. The rent-seeking behaviour they exhibited is crucially related to the high percentage of their exports that are raw materials (such as oil and gas), the high level of corruption, the development of the narcotics trade and chronic unemployment. The ability to address these problems will have an important impact on the stability of countries in the region. Thus there is a clear link between economics and security.

The governments of the Caspian Sea Region, which are in charge of resource-rich countries, are facing two major issues: how much of the potential income from the development of natural resources they should spend on the present generation and how much should be saved for the future; and how to adjust government spending in order to cushion the domestic economy from the unpredictability caused by variations in oil prices and revenue. Control over energy and other natural resources in the region is also a critical factor in the international relations of this new regional subsystem of states.

## Russian security policy and the southern periphery

There is no doubt that Russia sees the former Soviet states (with the exception of the Baltic states), and especially Central Asia, as its sphere of influence. However, this imperialist approach, though supported by the majority of the political elite, is not necessarily congruent with Russia's national interest. A lack of economic and financial resources, and constraints on Russia's current capability for the deployment of military forces across the whole of the former Soviet space, have placed severe limits on Russia's ability to realise its imperial ambitions.

Russia faces a number of problems in relation to this region - including problems of security, stability, geopolitical strategy, military infrastructure and energy. The inner-CIS borders remain unprotected, so that Russia's external border, in practice although not *de jure*, is the border of the former Soviet Union. For this reason Russia's national defence relies on forward bases and the protection of the borders of the former Soviet space. In particular Russia has been concerned about anti-Russian forces penetrating the region from Afghanistan. Secondly, Russia considers the Caucasus and Central Asia to be a zone of instability. Russia's military presence in the region is designed to deal with conflicts, prevent opposition forces from resorting to force in their struggle against existing governments, and to defend Russian citizens in those countries. Thirdly, Russia's geopolitical strategy is to seek to prevent other external actors - such as China, Turkey, Pakistan and Saudi Arabia - from gaining a foothold in the region and entering into alliances with the Central Asian countries. A fourth issue is the question of military infrastructure: this is problematic because there are still important military assets from Soviet times in the region, especially in air defence; and there is a spaceport in Baikonur that Russia wants to preserve and integrate into its military system. Finally, Russia wants to control energy resources throughout the former Soviet space.

In the face of the disintegration of the Soviet armed forces, Russia sought to establish a collective security regime in the former Soviet space by means of the Tashkent Treaty signed in May 1992. But there were two fundamental reasons why the Tashkent Treaty could not provide the basis for collective security in the former Soviet space. The first lay in the imbalance of power. The armed forces of the non-Russian former Soviet republics, especially the Central Asian states, had by 1992 dwindled to a small remnant, and most states (with the notable exception of Uzbekistan) were unwilling to invest significant resources in the military. Given that Russia had to supply the bulk of the forces for any significant crisis intervention in the region, no action could be expected to be taken unless it was considered to be in Russia's interest, and Russia was willing to bear the economic and human burden. The second problem was that there were no institutions in place that could guarantee or monitor the impartiality of any such intervention. The danger for the non-Russian states was that crisis intervention would become a tool for the promotion of Russian political interests throughout the former Soviet space. The non-Russian states found themselves in the paradoxical position that the guarantor of their security was also the greatest potential threat to their security; and the armed forces became a principal tool in ensuring the dominance of Russia's influence throughout Eurasia.

## Conflict and peacekeeping in the Caucasus and Central Asia

The peaceful dissolution of the Soviet Union was without doubt one of the most remarkable events in recent history. Nevertheless, the collapse of empire gave rise to regional conflicts; these resulted from the arbitrary territorial divisions inherited from the Soviet period, and from ethnic tensions that had long been suppressed. The Caucasus and Central Asia have experienced a wide range of conflicts, and this has shaped Russia's relations with the region, and especially its military involvement. The most serious conflict in the 1990s was the civil war in Tajikistan, in which there was considerable involvement by the Russian military, against the Islamic insurgents and in favour of President Rakhmonov. The conflict endured for a number of years, until in the end Russia supported a compromise with the opposition, resulting in the truce of 1997. At first the military were the dominant influence in Russian policy towards Tajikistan and other crisis regions of the South, but when military strategy proved inadequate, Russia's Foreign Minister Yevgeny Primakov gained greater influence. The crisis in Tajikistan also demonstrated the weakness of the collective security agreement, since the involvement of other Central Asian states was at best symbolic. This created a deep sense of insecurity in Uzbekistan, which saw itself as threatened by a possible overspill of the conflict from Tajikistan, and by the growth of Islamic opposition movements.

Other areas that have witnessed intense conflict include Armenia and Azerbaijan over Nagorno-Karabakh, Georgia and of course Dagestan and Chechnya. The conflict over Karabakh broke out in 1988 towards the end of the Soviet era, when the Karabakh region of Azerbaijan, which is mainly populated by Armenians, declared its intention to join the Armenian Soviet Socialist Republic. In 1992, after the dissolution of the USSR, this conflict erupted into war between the now independent states of Armenia and Azerbaijan. The fighting revealed that the balance of power was not as favourable to Azerbaijan as the Azeri government had initially believed. By the time a ceasefire was agreed in May 1994, Azerbaijan had effectively lost 20 per cent of its territory, and almost one million Azeri citizens has become internally displaced persons. Since then there have been negotiations on settling the dispute, but to no avail. The Azeri refusal to cede *de jure* sovereignty over the region has made it impossible to adopt any compromises on the administration of Karabakh, the status of its citizens and its relations to both Armenia and Azerbaijan. Russia and Turkey were the most important external players in this conflict. Turkey supported Azerbaijan and almost intervened directly following an Armenian attack on Nakhichevan in 1992. Its policy is designed to strengthen Turkish political influence in the Caucasus, and to share in the benefits from the construction of pipelines and the exploitation of hydrocarbon resources in the region. Although Russia seemed to support Armenia and clearly wanted to counter Turkish influence, it also needs to maintain influence in Azerbaijan. Greater stability is in Russia's interests, and Moscow is particularly concerned about the potential for the rise of radical Islam in Azerbaijan, especially among the people who were internally displaced during the fighting. The large oil reserves in Azerbaijan are another factor that gives it strategic importance from the Russian perspective. Despite President Putin's reputation for pragmatism, Russia is still actively frustrating a settlement of the conflict however; and this may not ultimately be in Russia's interest, as it perpetuates the potential for conflict and instability. Iran is another major external factor in this dispute, with 20 million Azerbaijanis living in Iran. Iran exercises considerable influence over the forces of Shia Islam in Azerbaijan, and this adds to the mix of potential causes of conflict in the region.

The most persistent conflict, however, is within the territory of the Russian Federation itself. The first Chechen war ended in ignominious defeat for Russia, and a settlement that was never fully accepted by Russia as the endstate of relations with the republic. The persistent internal strife in Chechnya meant that the republic failed to develop as an entity that was perceived as being capable of self-government. And then in 1999 two apartment blocks were blown up in Moscow, and Putin decided to respond with the direct and unrestrained use of military force, to deal with the terrorist threat that was said to emanate from the quasi-independent republic. Initially the second Chechen war served Putin well politically, but the failure to defeat the rebels has gradually turned it into a political liability. Terrorist attacks in Moscow itself have heightened anxiety in the population about this festering conflict.

The war in Chechnya is now being sold as part of the 'war against terror'. And although the West has continually criticised Russia for systematic human rights abuses in Chechnya, such criticism has become more muted after revelations that Islamic extremists from Pakistan and the Middle East were involved in the fighting, and in the light of Russia's support of the West in the war against terror.

One place where the terrorist threat escalated sharply was in the Pankisi Gorge in Georgia, which borders Chechnya and has been a place from which Chechen rebels have operated. On the basis of the alleged links of these rebels to Al-Qaeda, in 2002 the United States deployed some two hundred military instructors to Georgia to train the Georgian army and convert four battalions into a high state of combat readiness. The threat of Russian strikes against terrorists in the Pankisi Gorge was thus quickly defused. For the United States, the war against terror clearly has priority, and this has limited any pressure on Russia to modify its policies in the region. In the meantime Russia's policy towards the Caucasus has become more consistent and predictable, but it has failed to deal with the essential causes of the conflicts in the region. The fragile stability of the status quo hides the accumulation of problems, and a significant potential for conflict therefore persists. Western policy so far has also not made any significant contribution towards dealing with this situation.

### Energy resources in the Caspian region

International interest in Central Asia and the Caucasus has been heightened considerably by the substantial energy reserves in the region, especially in the Caspian area. Kazakhstan has the lion's share of oil reserves (27.6 billion barrels), followed by Azerbaijan (6.7 billion barrels). The total reserves are estimated to be 36.9 billion barrels, about 1.6 per cent of estimated world reserves of oil. Kazakhstan, Turkmenistan and Azerbaijan also have substantial reserves of gas. For Western Europe, the United States and China this potential for alternative sources of energy is significant, while the exploitation of oil reserves is also of major significance for multinational oil companies. The development of oil and gas production in the region has been faced with major structural and political problems however. There were structural problems resulting from the fact that the Caspian region is landlocked, and far from the world's major oil-consuming regions. Energy transport was consequently reliant on an extensive pipeline infrastructure through neighbouring countries. Substantial investment was required both to develop the oil fields and to build new pipelines.

> 'pipeline politics became an instrument of US strategic policy, designed to weaken Russia's hold in the region, and to prevent any relaxation in the isolation of Iran'

Russia's policy during the 1990s was based on seeking to exercise the greatest possible degree of control over energy resources in the former Soviet Union. This meant constraining the influence of the West and Western companies in the region, and limiting the amount of oil that Central Asian states, especially Kazakhstan, could transport through the Russian pipeline network. Kazakhstan was dependent on Russia not only for energy transport, but also for access to refineries, and this allowed Russia to dominate the financial arrangements for any transactions. The exploitation of Caspian oil was also constrained by a dispute over the demarcation of the Caspian and the ownership of reserves. For a number of years Russia obstructed resolution of this dispute, but in 2003 bilateral agreements between Russia, Azerbaijan and Kazakhstan were reached in relation to the oil fields in the Northern Caspian, on the basis of the 'Modified Median Line'. According to this principle, the median line is used to determine the boundary between two countries on the seabed, although modifications are agreed so that major oil or gas fields clearly belong to one country or the other. These agreements mean that (except for an immediate coastal strip) the waters can be regarded as common property. As for energy transport, a multiplicity of schemes for the construction of pipelines has resulted in a small cottage industry of speculation about various routes. However, few routes have commanded serious and sustained interest. The most important of the pipeline projects was the system that links the Tengiz and

*Eurasia at the crossroads*

Atyrau oil fields in Kazakhstan with the Russian Black Sea port of Novorossiysk constructed by the Caspian Pipeline Consortium (CPC) and capable of carrying 567,000 barrels per day.

The other major project is the Baku-Tbilisi-Ceyhan (BTC) pipeline. This project was launched in October 2002 with a projected cost of $3 billion, and a capacity of a million barrels per day at a cost of $3.2 per barrel; and it was opened in May 2005. The BTC project was of particular interest to the Turkish government, which was concerned about the increase that the pipeline projects would generate in oil tanker traffic through the environmentally sensitive Bosphorus. (The BTC pipeline bypasses the Bosphorus since it reaches the open sea at Ceyhan which is on Turkey's south-eastern Mediterranean coast.) This created a high level of controversy between Turkey and Russia, with Russia arguing that free passage through the Bosphorus waterway is guaranteed by the 1936 Montreux convention, and that the increase in oil tanker traffic could be dealt with through improvements in traffic control. Turkey brought the issue to the attention of various international bodies, including the International Maritime Organisation, and put its political support behind the BTC project. While Russia pursued the CPC project, the United States government actively backed the BTC routing. This was based on the view that the CPC pipeline would improve economic and political ties between the various countries of the region through which it ran, enable greater independence from Russia, and mitigate pressure for routing oil exports through Iran (whose Persian Gulf coast provides the shortest route to the open sea from the Caspian). Pipeline politics therefore became an instrument of US strategic policy towards the region, designed to weaken Russia's hold over its traditional sphere of influence, and to prevent any relaxation in the isolation of Iran.

China has also become a player in the exploitation of energy resources of the region. The principal motive for this is clear - China has become a net importer of oil and is seriously concerned about its excessive dependence on Middle East oil reserves. The export of energy is likely to be one of the principal elements of economic co-operation between China, Russia and Central Asia in the future. At the same time, co-operation with China gives Central Asian states, especially Kazakhstan, the possibility of reducing dependence on Russia. For China, energy co-operation with Kazakhstan can also serve to enhance its own political influence in the region at the expense of Russia. In 1997 China made two major investments in oil fields in Kazakhstan, and proposed a new pipeline project to deliver oil directly to China. For some time this project remained in abeyance, but in May 2004 Kazakh President Nursultan Nazarbayev signed an agreement with China for the construction of a 1240 km pipeline to the Chinese border.

The promise of untold riches from the Caspian has ultimately become rather muted. Although the estimated reserves are substantial, so are the costs of extraction and transportation. It has taken a long time for significant production to begin. Kazakhstan and Azerbaijan in particular are now beginning to see the benefits of their hydrocarbon reserves however. But it remains to be seen whether or not they will be able to manage this wealth in a productive manner, and to develop the other sectors of an economy that has been in severe decline in the post-Soviet transition.

With the more pragmatic and co-operative policies of Russia under Putin, some of the earlier political entanglements have begun to resolve themselves. While Iran still remains out in the cold, regional co-operation elsewhere has improved. But whatever else changes, hydrocarbon resources will continue to be of crucial importance for the economic future and political stability of the region, especially as world-wide demand is now so high.

## The geopolitics of Eurasia

The events of 9/11 afforded President Putin an opportunity to elevate US-Russian relations to the level of a new partnership and to override his critics at home, when he promised Russia's support in the fight against terror. There was much to gain for Russia. Until this moment Russia had figured relatively low in the priorities of the Bush administration. Russia needed a predictable international environment to the West, the continuation of the process of an orderly restructuring of the nuclear strategic relationship with the US, and continued economic support from the West. This path was resumed once Russia's violation of human rights in Chechnya was incorporated into the context of the war on terror. Furthermore, the US war against the Taliban and Al-Qaeda dealt with Russia's most serious external security threat, namely infiltration from Afghanistan by the Taliban and other Islamic extremists. In particular, it deprived the Islamic Movement of Uzbekistan and other insurgent movements of their base in Afghanistan. In turn, the US benefited greatly from Russian intelligence about Afghanistan, the activities of the Taliban and the location of Al-Qaeda training camps. The United States also needed to base forces in Central Asia, and states in the region, especially Tajikistan and Uzbekistan, were keen to host American forces. Strictly speaking the United States did not need Russia's permission for this, but serious opposition by the Russian government would have made the decision more difficult for the governments of Tajikistan and Kyrgyzstan. Despite some misgivings in Moscow, Putin made a virtue out of the necessity of acquiescing to the basing of US forces on former Soviet territory. Russia not only supplied intelligence and humanitarian air corridors, but also provided arms for the anti-Taliban Northern Alliance, which played a key role in the US campaign in Afghanistan.

Thus Russia has benefited enormously from the war against terror. But its relationship with the United States can scarcely be described as a strategic partnership. Not only did Moscow oppose Washington on the conflict with Iraq, a matter of vital strategic interest; even worse from the point of view of the United States, it has developed a long-term partnership with Iran to supply nuclear technology. In Eurasia itself, the United States is considered simultaneously a partner and a rival. Russia has been perturbed by the 'orange revolutions' in Ukraine, Georgia and Kyrgyzstan, which have brought democracy and thus disturbed the cosy arrangements that Moscow had with the governments of these countries. The violent repression of similar public protests in Uzbekistan forced the regime in Moscow to reveal once again its true authoritarian colours, and the United States was given notice to remove its forces from Uzbek territory.

The future looks brighter for Eurasia today than it did in the early years after the dissolution of the Soviet Union. Having gone through the bitter years of economic depression, the region is beginning to do better, in significant part due to the high global demand for oil and gas. The bitter civil war in Tajikistan has been settled, and the Taliban threat has been dealt with. Nevertheless, Eurasian countries have only just begun to deal with the challenges of governance and economic development that they face. Given the present geopolitical importance of the region, there is a crucial role that the United States and European countries can play - as long as issues of governance and human rights are not ignored, as they have been in the past, to further broader geopolitical interests.

**Soundings** is now freely available online to all subscribers

Benefits include:

- Document to document linking using live references, for fast, reliable access to wider, related literature.
- Journal content that is fully searchable, across full text, abstracts, titles, TOCs and figures.
- Live links to and from major Abstract and Indexing resources to aid research.
- The ability to conduct full-text searching across multiple journals, giving you a wider view of the research that counts.
- Powerful TOC alerting services that keep you up to date with the latest research.

Set up access now at: www.ingentaselect.com/register.htm
and follow the online instructions*

Subscription Enquiries: help@ingenta.com
*Access is provided by Ingenta Select, an Ingenta website

## SPECIAL OFFER TO NEW SUBSCRIBERS

First time individual subscribers are entitled to a £30 subscription for the first year

**Subscription rates 2006 (3 issues)**

Individual subscriptions:     UK £35      Rest of the World £45
Institutional subscriptions:  UK £75      Rest of the World £85

To subscribe, send your name and address and payment (cheque or credit card), stating which issue you want the subscription to start with, to Soundings, Lawrence & Wishart Subs, PO Box 7701, Latchingdon, Chelmsford, CM3 6WL. Alternatively, you can e-mail us at landw@btinternet.com or visit our website at www.lwbooks.co.uk and navigate to the shopping basket (www.lwbooks.co.uk/products.php?cat=2).

# Three poems

## Poem of the Nile

*Prelude*
Walls climb the ivy
And Khartoum, poised on its unamputated foot
    Singing
Will the Nile ever escape into sleep?
We were the most loving of lovers, children trickling from us
What name do you give me?
I call you Presence of Earth. Come closer then.
What will be the taste of grief?
......................
    And we parted!

*Sura*
The Nile flows quietly ...
    Seeping through the city's silence
        And the burning sorrows of villages.

Now friends no longer exchange greetings each morning
    No longer recognize each other.
        Everywhere one sees them, these one-time prophets,

Poverty-stricken, sipping their tea, their tears,
    Speechless.
        They hide death in their fraying clothes,

And all they can say to our children is: patience.
    They fade into the trees, commit suicide
        At night, derive from alcohol

Their arguments, embark on futile wars
    With their women, give up
        Their prayers, then disappear.

Walls climb the ivy
And Khartoum, sitting in a café
    Smoking
In the dark you can't tell apart
Muggers from those whose journeys they'd cut short.
We were lovers, looking for our children
Who were breaking into bakeries, stealing fire
From the ovens' throats.
What name do you give me?
I call you earth's Fiery Anger. So rise up.
What will be the taste of ashes?
……………………..
    And we parted!

*Sura*
Fire is the opposite of Water
And Smoke is a memory that prepares us only for ash.
Water is the opposite of Fire
And the waves are like maps, rippling across the land.
And the girl? She is somewhere between this heart and this knife…

City - you're a handful of grains of wheat, tucked
Into the purses of usurers and slave-traders.
And the black men

Are approaching, approaching. River Nile
    To what deserts are you taking my reflections? You depart
        And I stand among the horses, by your gate,

*Three Poems*

And my soul would embark on a holy journey too,
    For the silence suspended between us
        Is a language floating among the ruins of a beautiful,
vanished past.

O River Nile, father
Were the trees merely windows reflecting women's sorrows,
Or have your waters shattered their images,
Drowned the history of women,
And painted forever their meadows the colour of poverty?
Poverty invades the children's playgrounds, leaving
Them silent, accursed, their heritage
Only anger and disbelief.

The Nile opens his arms
Speaks to the migrant birds
    Falls silent
Reigns
    And never sleeps
    Never sleeps

The Nile drinks dry the desert's tavern,
Gets drunk on dumps of toxic waste,
Must survive in the city, falling apart
Each night, rising up through its history
    And never sleeps
    Never sleeps

The drums began with the sun
And its light filtered songs that entered into the pores of the soul.
In the river's shallows boats sheltered from toil and wind.
Now the carnivals of the blacks take fire
And the Nile has burst through the layers of time.

And, see, the kingdom of Maroe appears
And the face of the Nubian lover
Who walks among the sorrows of the waterwheels
Searching for warriors among the horses.
Where does the line of ancestral blood begin
And when does the blood loss reach its climax,
O King Bia, enthroned ruler of Kush,
A kingdom unravelling in bitter silence?

Shout at the horses, and let
The waters ready themselves.
Let the maps explode. How can the land be lost
When the future belongs to the Nile?

The Nile knows of the disgrace of cities
That have vanished.
Knows of the old times
Yet never speaks.
It is the Nile …
Generations will pass, and there will always be children
Lingering on its banks,
Waiting
For it all to end.

*Al-Saddiq Al-Raddi*
*translated by Mark Ford and Hafiz Kheir (with thanks to the Poetry Translation Centre at The School of African and Oriental Studies www.poetrytranslation.soas.ac.uk)*

# Anne Glyd,
## her book 1656, offered by her servant, poor Colly

A stone growing in gall of an old ox,
And the same quantity of a dead man's skull
That comes to an untimely end:

Mix as much as will lie on two pence
And give the child the hair that appears
Between the hinder legs of a her-bear

Boiled in brandy till the brandy be consumed –
Lay it warm to the soles of the feet.
Take the liver and heart of a hare

And bake it in a pot in an oven
After brown bread is drawn,
Then take in motherwort,

Which if not to be had you make shift without,
And mix it into a powder,
And let there be twice as much

Powder of hare as of motherwort:
Let the party drink
As much as will lie on a shilling

In a wineglass of black cherry water
A week before the full of the moon
And a week before new moon.

This with God's blessing has cured many.
Take a cloth from the woman that floods
And wring it into a glass of beer:

This may be given in a posset
When they have the smallpox.
If a woman that is much weakened with her courses

Doth eat the same, or let the same
Run into a hole made in the ground
With a three-squared stake,

The same stake immediately after
Being put in or drove into the same hole,
And so remain therein unremoved,

Her said flux will cease, being thought before incurable.
To cause pains when a woman cannot be delivered,
Let her drink a good porringer of her husband's water:
(Proved myself). Take a cloth
That another woman wears when her courses are upon her,
And it coming wet with her courses from her,

Lay it upon the belly of the woman in travail,
It will cause pain.
Take a handful of herb grace,
A pint of honey, hot and well clarified,

With a great spoonful of pepper bruised.
Also she must eat every day
Raisins of the sun.
Let her eat heartily.

If you see not the party mend
At the end of ten weeks,
She shall be perfect whole, by God's grace.

Make thin bowls of lead fit to cover the breast or wen,
And when you do lay it to the breast, warm it a little,
And so whelm it upon the breast and make it fast

That it remove not, and let it lie
As you feel occasion. An honest woman
Revealed this who had proved it to be true.

And she learned it of a poor woman
That required alms at her door.

*Medbh McGuckian*

# White farmhouse
*after* Colin Middleton

Colin Middleton knew that he was dying
And fitted all the colours he had ever used
Into his last painting, a white farmhouse
Among drumlins, the gable and chimneys
White, the corn harvested by his palette-knife,
A besmirching of corn poppy, cornflower,
One blue-black spinney, triangles of sunlight
Disappearing between Octobery hedges,
Another farmhouse in the distance like home.
Colin Middleton was a friend of mine
When I was young. How can I count the colours?
There are no doors or windows in the building,
No outhouses. I name the picture for myself.
Titles, said Duchamp, are invisible colours.

Michael Longley

# Detente at the Flying Horse

## Barry Gifford

Roy had a job changing tyres and pumping gas two days a week after school at the Flying Horse service station on the corner of Peterson and Western. This was during the winter when he was sixteen. The three other weekday afternoons and also on Saturdays he worked at the Red Hot Ranch, a hot dog and hamburger joint. Roy had taken the gas station job in addition to his long-standing employment at the Ranch because his mother had had her hours reduced as a receptionist at Winnemac Hospital. His sister had just begun grammar school and they needed the money. Roy knew that his mother was considering getting married again - for what would be the fourth time - as a way to support them, a move he wanted desperately to avert or, at the least, delay. None of his mother's marriages had been successful, as even she would admit, other than two of them having produced Roy and his little sister. They were her treasures, she assured them; their existence had made her otherwise unfortunate forays into matrimony worthwhile.

Domingo and Damaso Parlanchín, two Puerto Rican brothers, owned the Flying Horse. They were good mechanics, originally from San Juan, who had worked for other people for fifteen years and saved their money so that they could buy their own station. They were short, chubby, good-humoured men in their forties, constantly chattering to each other in rapid Spanish. The Parlanchín brothers paid Roy a dollar an hour and fifty cents for each tyre he changed, half of what it cost the customer. Damaso could patch a flat faster than Roy could get it off the car and back on again, and do it without missing a beat in the running conversation with his brother. Domingo was the better mechanic of the two, the more analytically adept. Damaso was superior at handling the customers, able to convince them they needed an oil change or an upgrade of their tyres.

It was no fun changing tyres in January in Chicago. The temperature often fell well below zero degrees Fahrenheit and icy winds off the lake scorched Roy's perpetually scraped knuckles and cut fingers. Prying loose frozen lug nuts was Roy's greatest difficulty until Domingo showed him how to use an acetylene torch to heat the bolts before attempting to turn them with a tyre iron. 'Cuidado con la lanzallamas,' Domingo told Roy.

One snowy afternoon about a quarter to four, just before dark, a black and white Buick Century ka-bumped into the station on its rims and stopped. All four tyres were flat. Roy could see that they were studded with nails. Two burly men in dark blue overcoats and Homburg hats sat in the front seat. They did not get out, so Roy went over to the driver's side window and nodded at him. The man rolled down the window. He was about forty-five years old, had a three-day beard and a four inch-long scar across the left side of his lips. The man in the passenger seat looked just like the driver, except for the scar.

'How fast fix?' asked the driver.
'It looks like you need four new tyres, sir,' said Roy.
'Not possible fix?'
'I'll ask my boss, but I doubt it. You're riding on your rims. We'll have to check if they're bent.'
'Go ask boss.'

Roy trudged through the thick, wet snow to the garage, where Domingo and Damaso were working over a transmission on a 1956 Ford Apache pick-up.

'There's a guy here who needs four tyres replaced. Looks like he drove over a bed of nails.'
'Tell him he can to leave it,' said Damaso.
'And coming back at siete horas,' Domingo added.

The wind ripped into Roy's face when he removed his muffler from around his mouth to convey this information to the driver of the Buick. Roy's eyes stung; they watered as he waited for the man to respond.

*Detente at the Flying Horse*

'Cannot they fix now?'

'No,' said Roy, 'we're pretty backed up.'

The driver spoke to his companion in a language Roy could not readily identify. The wind whined and shrieked, making it difficult for Roy to hear anything else.

'We wait,' the driver told him. 'Can fix sooner.'

Roy shook his head. 'Maybe you'd better try another station. But you'll damage your wheels.'

The man produced a fifty dollar bill and shoved it at Roy. He held it between two black leather-gloved fingers. 'This extra. Okey dokey?' he said. 'You give boss.'

Roy accepted the bill, marched back to the garage and handed it to Domingo.

'The guy says this is on top of the cost of replacing the tyres, if we can do it now.'

'Tell him drive in muy despacio,' said Domingo.

After the man had done this, following Damaso's signals to pull up into the other bay and onto the lift, Damaso told the men to get out of the car.

'We stay in,' said the driver.

'No es posible raise car with you inside. Insurance no good if you fall.'

The driver held out another fifty. Damaso took it. He nodded to Domingo, who activated the lift.

'Lock doors!' Damaso shouted up at the men. 'And no move!'

Roy pumped gas for several customers while the Parlanchín brothers worked on the Buick. The sky had gone dark and snow kept falling. Before the Buick pulled out of the station on four new Bridgestones, it stopped next to Roy. The driver rolled down his window.

'Yes, sir?' said Roy. 'Is everything okay?'
'All okey dokey,' replied the driver. 'You young boy, work hard bad weather. How much Spanish men pay you?'
'Buck an hour and two bits a flat.'
'Slave wage,' said the man. 'Now 1962. Take.'

The driver extended toward Roy his black gloved left hand between two fingers of which protruded another fifty-dollar bill. Roy took the money and stuffed it into one of the snap pockets of his brown leather jacket.

'Thank you,' he said. 'Where are you guys from?'
'You know Iron Curtain?'
'I've heard of it.'
'We are from behind.'

After the Buick had gone, Roy went into the garage.

'Strange hombres, si?' said Domingo.
'The driver gave me a tip,' Roy told him. 'I don't know why, though.'
'He give us a hundred extra,' said Damaso.
'The Buick had diplomatic license plates,' Roy said. 'They're Russians, I think.'
'Must be they are trying to be more friendly,' Domingo suggested, 'since they been forced to take missiles out of Cuba.'

When Roy was eleven, he remembered, his mother had had a boyfriend from Havana, a conga drummer named Raul Repilado. She had met him in Coral Gables, Florida, when she and her third husband, Sid Wade, the father of Roy's sister, were vacationing at the Biltmore. Raul Repilado's band, the Orquesta Furioso, was appearing at the hotel. Raul had come to Chicago a couple of times to see Roy's mother, the last time during the winter. Before leaving, the conguero declared that he would never come back to such a terribly cold place, even for a beautiful woman. Roy couldn't wait to tell his mother that he'd made an extra fifty bucks that day.

# REVIEWS

# Prozac on paper
John Jordan

Rebecca Solnit, *Hope in the Dark: The Untold History of People Power*, Canongate £7.99

I have rarely felt so dark. For years, when people asked me what I did, rather than explain my complex status as a professional amateur, I would simply say 'I'm a pathological optimist'. Today, as I pushed through the crowds fighting their way through London's Regent Street sales with their bulging carrier bags, filled to the brim with empty promises and mountains of plastic, I realised that I could no longer call myself that. I realised that I had lost something; the very thing that had propelled me over the last decade had faded, slipped away. A powerful kind of hope had kept me (hyper) active in the burgeoning anti-capitalist networks, it had kept me awake at night putting the last touches to propaganda, had provided me with courage on the streets when being tear-gassed by faceless cops, it had taken me across the world to share inspirations and tactics - Seattle, Chiapas, Quebec, Genoa, Argentina. Everywhere I had seen signs of hope, in every gesture, every anecdote, every example of autonomous living I had seen new worlds coming into being, I had seen a new politics of becoming emerge, a politics which was changing the world without the illusion of wanting to take power, without participating in the fantasy that controlling the state had much to do with taking back control of one's everyday life.

I'm not sure why I was drifting into this space of debilitating despair. Perhaps it was reading Derrick Jensen's *A Language Older than Words*, his terrifyingly touching memoir cum tirade against the endemic violence and barbarism of capitalism. Perhaps it was seeing all the work we had put into the radical resistance to the G8 summit this summer blown away the next day by the London bombs. Perhaps it was seeing the 'No Future' fires of the French suburbs fanning further racism and repression. Perhaps it was Hurricane Katrina, or the slowing gulf stream, permanent war or bird flu. Perhaps it was participating in a weekend workshop entitled 'Apocalypse Soon', which convinced me that peak oil was going to throw us into what James Howard Kunstler calls the 'Long emergency', the tremendous trauma and economic collapse which will go hand in hand with the end of the age of cheap oil. Imagining the end of the world, in other words, had become easier than imagining changing it.

'The Apocalypse is always easier to imagine than the strange circuitous routes to what actually comes next', writes Rebecca Solnit in *Hope in the Dark: The Untold History of People Power*, her extraordinarily poetic manifesto for new ways of thinking about how radical social change comes about. It seems I had fallen into the typical leftist trap that Solnit describes as the 'mutual wailing about how bad everything (is)', and had forgotten that what had kept my hope alive for so long was a profound belief in the unexpected nature of history and activism. This is a state of mind that *Hope in the Dark* beautifully illustrates through myriad stories of 'victories and possibilities'. ' Hope', she writes, 'is the story of uncertainty, of coming to terms with the risk involved in not knowing what comes next, which is more demanding than despair, and in a way, more frightening. And immeasurably more rewarding.'

Since the book (which, at 170 pages, exists more within the sadly little-practised tradition of radical pamphleteering) came out in the US last year, I have been passing battered copies of it to numerous activists and rebels, many of whom have lost confidence in the movement of movements that had promised so much before 9/11. I have often described it not only as 'Prozac on paper', but as perhaps the only book that accurately captures the radical spirit and philosophy of this diverse global network of resistance. Theorising an exhilarating, non-linear way of understanding social change and redefining hope as a practice of the present - of the imagination and of action rather than a projection into some distant abstracted unknown future - the book seamlessly merges the spirits of anarchism, Zapatismo, Buddhism, complexity theory, ecology, feminism, Foucault, Deleuze and Guattari with the passionate intensity and grace that we have become used to with Solnit's writings. (See for example *Wanderlust: A History of Walking*, Verso 2002 and *Motion Studies: Time, Space and Eadweard Muybridge*, Bloomsbury 2004.)

The book challenges the binary and oppositional thinking that is still so inherent within protest movements (and society at large). Dichotomies between the personal and the political, 'us' and 'them', activist and non-activist, are clearly outmoded ways of thinking in movements that emphasise processes, continuum, relationships, systems and networks rather than the linear march of history and political parties. But perhaps the greatest challenge Solnit presents us with is to hold the paradoxical thought in our head that the world is both getting worse and better at the same time - the ice caps may be melting and yet salmon are returning to numerous rivers across the world; religious fundamentalism may be re-emerging but thirty years ago gay marriage was inconceivable. Activists take for granted many of the changes that they themselves helped bring about and yet they beat themselves with the rod of perfection - for radicals nothing is ever enough. But saying 'everything is going to hell' is merely an inverted version of 'everything is going to be fine', and what we have to do is to see the darkness of the future as the most wonderful realm of possibility and remember that every act of resistance counts precisely because we can never predict its effectiveness. In fact by approaching direct action as a force that is indirect, and never perfect, we create the grounds for hope and open ourselves up to be astonished by what might happen. Drifting through tales from the anti-nuclear movements to the Spanish Civil War, from Seattle to the Zapatista uprising, Solnit beautifully lays out the meandering pathways of a continually unfolding and unfinished history. She points out how the successes of activism are frequently invisible, because our victories are often what *didn't* happen - the new roads programme was never built, a generation of nuclear weapons was scrapped, the hemispherical free trade agreement was never signed.

A strange kind of antithetical companion to *Hope in the Dark* is Malcolm Gladwell's *The Tipping Point*, currently WH Smith's 'Number two Business Book of the Month'. Analysing the seemingly magic moment when ideas and small gestures take on epidemic proportions and spread like wildfire, the book is being touted amongst the trend-setters, PR agencies and marketing gurus as a manual for predicting the unpredictable, so that they can push brands and products into the minds and shopping bags of consumers. Gladwell gives us rules to explain the counter-intuitive ways ideas spread, whilst Solnit uses rich stories; she constantly reminds us that every revolution began in the imagination, and that as artists and activists our work is to make this world a place where everyone is a producer rather than simply a consumer of meaning. Perhaps next time I battle my way through Regent Street I will try to remember Solnit's battle cry, 'To hope is to gamble. It's to bet on the future, on your desires, on the possibility that an open heart and uncertainty is better than gloom and safety. To hope is dangerous, and yet it is the opposite of fear, for to live is to risk'. And I will eject myself from the ease of despair back into the wild adventure that recognises that anything could happen, and whether I act or not has everything to do with it.

# Naming the enemy

## Jeremy Gilbert

Retort, *Afflicted Powers: Capital and Spectacle in a New Age of War*, Verso £9.99; David Harvey, *A Brief History of Neoliberalism*, Oxford University Press £14.99

*Afflicted Powers*, a book written by the San Francisco Bay Area collective Retort, has already received a good deal of attention in the intellectual left press (see, for example, Kate Soper's commentary in *Radical Philosophy* 135). This is perhaps surprising considering the relative obscurity of its source, although it is maybe less so when we take into account the persuasive power of the Verso publicity machine and the obvious timely and urgent nature of the questions which the book addresses. *A Brief History of Neoliberalism* is the latest work from David Harvey, one of the foremost exponents of Marxist social analysis writing in English today. What the two works share is a determination to understand and expose the lineaments of neoliberalism, understood as a coherent and aggressive political project driven by Washington and backed by American commercial and military power, and obeying the most basic and irreducible logic of capitalist accumulation. The Bush administration's policy of military conquest and the general authoritarian programme implemented under the rubric of the 'war on terror' poses some problems for any account of 'neoliberalism' which understands it exclusively in terms of its tendency to open up markets. It isn't immediately obvious why a policy aimed at promoting free commerce and rolling back the state should resort to such measures. In different but overlapping ways, however, these two books demonstrate the continuity between the different elements of this programme.

Harvey's analysis is the more predictable, if nonetheless essential. Charting neoliberalism's history as an effective political history from the Pinochet coup of 1971, through the New York City budgetary crisis of the mid 1970s and the accession to power of Deng Xiao Ping, Margaret Thatcher and Ronald Reagan, up to the present day, it is acute, precise and global in its scope. Specifically, Harvey identifies neoliberalism as a programme whose key point of consistency is its overriding objective of constituting, reconstituting and augmenting the class power of Capital, which had been severely weakened in the middle decades of the twentieth century by the successes of Communism, Keynesianism and Social Democracy. This is an old argument but one which bears endless repetition in the current climate: the contradiction between liberal individualism and authoritarian, militaristic state action is only apparent if we ignore the fact that both are deployed selectively in the interests of capital accumulation. An argument made strongly by both of these books is that what Retort (after Marx) call 'primitive accumulation' and Harvey calls 'accumulation by dispossession' has always been a fundamental operation of capitalism. Commodification - the basic logic of capitalist social relations - can only begin or proceed by making commodities out of resources which were once held (at least potentially) in common: this is as true of the common lands of eighteenth-century England and the schools of contemporary Britain as it is of the state-owned oil fields of Baathist Iraq.

Harvey is much weaker when he attempts to comment on the cultural implications and conditions of possibility of the neoliberal programme. The chapter on the 'construction of consent', despite its Gramscian terminology, makes no reference at all to the extensive literature on the precise cultural-political conditions under which Thatcher and Reagan won hegemony by putting together unlikely social coalitions for their combined programmes of economic liberalisation and (largely rhetorical) social conservatism. So, for example, the extent to which anxieties over immigration and crime formed the context for the 'Thatcher revolution' is simply overlooked.

This is not simply a question of a short book giving necessarily brief attention to local details: the inability to think through the political complexity of contemporary culture with anything like the rigour with which it addresses economic issues is typical of this kind of classical Marxism. The final pages of the book are where this weakness fully reveals itself. Forcing himself - bravely - to move out of the mode of declarative condemnation in order to address the possibilities for resistance to neoliberal hegemony, Harvey is unable to muster anything but the most half-hearted enthusiasm for oppositional tendencies, such as the World Social Forum, which do not conform to the classical ideal of class struggle rooted in the Labour movement.

Most disappointingly, in the last couple of pages we have to sit through Harvey citing himself (in 1989) citing that most complacent of tenured Marxists, Terry Eagleton, giving a typically lazy and misleading account of J. F. Lyotard's *The Postmodern Condition*, which is condemned, as it has so often been, for its supposed advocacy of epistemological nihilism. I've lost count of the number of times I've come across Lyotard's arguments in this book thus misrepresented, as defenders of left orthodoxy shoot blindly at the messenger rather than confronting the questions that he raises. The fact is, like it or not, that Lyotard's 1979 essay accurately predicted the shape of contemporary education, information culture and the knowledge economy at a moment when only the dimmest glimmerings of the internet future could be discerned, and to see him dismissed at third hand by a scholar as generally rigorous as Harvey is almost as depressing as his account of the long march of neoliberalism. Ultimately, Harvey's only faint hope for the future lies in his observation that neoliberalism is, on its own terms, in deep crisis, as indicated by the currently massive financial deficit of the US government. This again is typical of a Marxian tradition which is brilliant at describing capitalism, but useless at grappling with the political problem of why people participate in it and how they might be persuaded not to.

Retort's cultural analysis is certainly more idiosyncratic, and the focus of *Afflicted Powers* is quite different, although there are significant overlaps with Harvey's book. Retort use the suggestive phrase 'military neoliberalism' to describe the current programme of the US, but their wider argument is motivated in part by a dissatisfaction with the idea that the war in Iraq can be explained simply in terms of a project to appropriate oil reserves and even to create a bridgehead for the 'free' market in the Middle East. Instead they draw on the legacy of Situationism - in particular Debord's concept of 'the Spectacle' - to interrogate the questions of just why '9/11' was so traumatic for the American psyche and why America persists in an unwavering support for Israel which has long since ceased to be useful to its project of global hegemony.

The problems inherent in this manoeuvre should be immediately apparent. The trouble with the term 'Spectacle' was always its particularly unhelpful combination of generality and specificity: on the one hand 'Spectacle' is simply a name for the reified totality of phenomena in advanced capitalist societies; on the other hand it designates that totality only in its aspect as an ephemeral and superficial mask for the reality of capitalist social relations. Thankfully Retort retain little of the moralism which infuses Debord's account, but it then becomes entirely unclear how the notion of 'Spectacle' does anything that terms like 'ideology', 'collective fantasy' and 'political imaginary' do not do - other than to obfuscate the complex relationships between different elements of ideological and psychic processes which those terms try to specify. The final sections of the book offer a very intriguing account of the roots of contemporary Islamic militancy in Leninist vanguardism (although one wonders if the traditional Situationist antipathy for the latter isn't motivating this history more than any exhaustive archival research), and the specific modernity of contemporary 'terrorism'. It's all useful and interesting stuff, but it's also amazing that these guys manage not even to acknowledge John Gray's *Al-Quaeda and what it Means to Be Modern*, which makes almost exactly the same argument from within the tradition of conservative scepticism.

Overall, the gambit of *Afflicted Powers*, like that of Hardt and Negri's recent work, is to sacrifice detailed analytical or conceptual rigour for readability and the deployment of terminologies which might be readily adopted by non-academic activists. Rather like Hardt & Negri, however, the relative successes and failures of their arguments reveal the limitations of this approach. Both *Afflicted Powers* and *Multitude* (and, for that matter, *A Brief History of Neoliberalism*) deal with the idea of perpetual war and ongoing militarisation as the general condition of either capitalist modernity as such or the current phase of neoliberal expansion, and all treat this particular topic in a useful and persuasive manner. Where many of their arguments start to fall apart, however, is at the point where they attempt to map the complex reality of contemporary capitalism in terms whose simplifying generality ('Empire', 'Spectacle') hides more than it reveals. It is true that radical theory has today become difficult and complex for many non-specialists to engage with, but so has contemporary capitalism. In the end, there is no substitute for the difficult work of keeping up with this complexity in our own analyses of neoliberalism, capitalism and their cultural and political conditions of possibility, and generalising hypotheses do as much harm as good in the process of trying to map this difficult terrain. In the end, then, it is Harvey's specific and detailed account of the neoliberal project which, despite its crude cultural politics, offers the most usable route through, and perhaps even out of, the current impasse of liberal democracy.

# Feminism and economics

## Sue Himmelweit

*Sue Himmelweit outlines some of the main features of feminist work in economics.*

During the 1990s, finance ministries throughout the world took increasing control of all aspects of public policy and economics became the dominant discourse of policy-makers. During the same decade, feminist economics started to make its mark. In 1992, the International Association for Feminist Economics (IAFFE) was founded. IAFFE now has about six hundred members, in forty countries, holds an annual conference and organises sessions on feminist economics at a number of mainstream economics conferences. Since 1995 it has published its own highly respected academic journal *Feminist Economics*. Feminist economics has been described as the economic theory behind gender mainstreaming.[1] And as the influence of economic discourse has spread to other areas of public policy, feminist economics has become relevant to an increasingly wide area of policy.

Advocates of feminist economics see it as a critique of mainstream economics, concerned with uncovering the underlying gender dimensions of economic processes, and as a political project, 'a rethinking of the discipline of economics for the purpose of improving women's position'.[2] They also see it as a better way of doing economics; its insights and methods would improve the analysis and policy conclusions made by mainstream economists. These improvements would include not only replacing gender blindness by a rigorous attention to

---

1. Jill Rubery, 'Reflections on gender mainstreaming: An example of feminist economics in action?', *Feminist Economics*, 11(3), 2005.
2. Myra H. Strober, 'Rethinking Economics Through a Feminist Lens', *American Economic Review*, 84(2), 1994, p143.

gender, but also broadening the scope of economics to include domains that have traditionally been seen as outside economics, such as unpaid domestic work and all forms of caring. The practice of feminist economics also introduces new methods - such as talking to economic actors - and new data sources - such as ethnographic data - previously neglected by economists. Finally, insights from feminist economics should enable economists to become more methodologically self-conscious through becoming aware of where their own discipline is situated, how its existing hierarchies and conventions work against feminist analysis, and how existing practice supports the (gender unequal) status quo.

As in many other disciplines, the feminist critique of economics developed in stages: from combating discrimination in the profession, to criticising the practice of economics as sexist or gender blind, to engaging with the androcentrism of its fundamental tenets and methods. Initially this was mainly to point out the way in which women were omitted from analysis, for example when data was given only for men, without the omission of women being justified or even acknowledged in some cases. Feminists pointed out that economics operated on the implicit assumption that men were normal and women different. Later feminist critiques focused on the gender blindness of economists who ignore gender difference even where it has a material effect on the topic at hand. For example, in attempting to explain differences in wage rates, many articles made no mention of the fact that a substantial proportion of women's employment in the UK is part-time, while men's tends to be full-time. More recently feminist economists have moved on to wide-ranging critiques of the androcentrism of mainstream economics, focusing on its assumptions, methods, findings and policy prescriptions.

These wide-ranging critiques require a 'thicker' conception of gender than the relatively thin one used in earlier stages, in which differential effects by gender are uncovered by splitting populations into men and women and examining the differences.[3] Gender analysis using such a thin conception of gender now occurs regularly in mainstream economics. For example, there have been numerous attempts to explain the differences between men's and women's pay or labour

---

3. Ingrid Robeyns, 'Is there a Feminist Economic Methodology?' uses these different conceptions of gender to distinguish feminist from mainstream economics, available at www.ingridrobeyns.nl/Downloads/method.pdf.

market participation rates by using multiple regression analysis, a method of taking a large number of variables into account to see which differences between men and women - for example in education, experience or hours of work - have significant effects. Invariably a residual is found, a difference that cannot be explained by the factors considered in the analysis. Mainstream economists would see this residual as the only specific gender effect. Some are willing to label that residual 'discrimination'; others see it as due to 'unobserved factors', that future work might show also not to be due to 'gender'. Feminist economists point out that 'explaining' gender differences in pay or labour participation rates as the effects of differences in other factors simply begs the question of why there are gender differences in those other factors.

The 'thicker' conception of gender in feminist economics recognises structural differences in the positions of men and women in the economy and the forms of agency through which those structural differences are reproduced. Gender is seen as a source not just of incidental differences but of structured inequalities. In the thin conception, gender is a side issue that has little bearing on how the economy as a whole works, nor on how economics is carried out. The thicker conception of gender makes it a systematic, structuring factor for the whole economy and consequently for how we think about economics.

## What is economics?

Much more than other social science disciplines, economics is dominated by one single mainstream approach, 'neo-classical' economics, which attempts to explain economic phenomena in terms of one universally applicable model of human behaviour, known even before feminism gave the name an ironic edge, as 'rational economic man' (REM).[4] Rational economic man has a set of preferences over all possible states he could be in, which he uses to decide what to do, choosing whichever of the currently available choices he most prefers. Theorising based on alternative assumptions, or trying to challenge the idea that everything can be explained by a single model of individual decision-making, are seen simply as 'not economics' (though economists have shown no reticence in attempting to use the axiomatic foundations of REM to 'explain' phenomena traditionally the subject matter of other disciplines, such as criminal behaviour, marriage patterns

---

4. For more on this see Edward Fullbrook's 'Post-autistic economics', in *Soundings* 29.

and the formation of political parties[5]).

So feminist economists have had to challenge not only the content but also the definition and boundaries of the discipline. One definition found in many standard textbooks is that economics is the *study of choice in conditions of scarcity* - broadly how people make choices when they cannot have everything that they want. Another more abstract definition, which comes to much the same thing, is that economics is the *study of rational behaviour* i.e. the study of Rational Economic Man, and his method of decision-making. Most feminist economics would criticise the notion of a methodological definition, particularly since such definitions operate to validate the exclusive use of a particular set of sparse assumptions in building formal models that are highly simplified accounts of the world (though they usually require complex mathematics for working out their results). Feminist economists tend to favour a more problem-oriented approach to definition.

Two less abstract, more content-oriented definitions of economics are that it is the *study of markets*, or more broadly that it is the *study of production, distribution and exchange*. Both these definitions have been criticised by feminists for not taking sufficient account of factors that lie outside their domain but nevertheless have bearing on much that goes on within it - for example, gender norms over caring that impact on men's and women's engagement in the labour market. These definitions are seen as androcentric, because what they exclude is not a question of chance, and includes much that women do. In particular women's lives are spent largely on non-market activities and are frequently concerned not with the production of things but the reproduction of people. To omit these aspects of women's lives is a serious problem, even in work solely focused on the traditional concerns of economists, for the time and resources that go into unpaid and reproductive activities and the results of these activities have significant effects on the market economy, and on how goods of all types are produced, distributed and exchanged.

Julie Nelson argues that economics should be the study of the 'provisioning' of the necessaries of life, thus extending a content-oriented definition of economics

---

5. The Nobel prize-winner Gary Becker is most renowned for these 'imperialistic' attempts to spread the use of REM, most notably for feminists in 'Theory of Marriage', *Journal of Political Economy*, (part I) 81,1973 and (part II) 82, 1974; and his *Treatise on the Family*, enlarged edition, Harvard University Press 1991.

to include the contributions that women tend to make, including childbirth, caring and domestic and community work.[6] Others argue that if economics is concerned with constrained choice, it should focus more on the nature of those constraints, and should include other socially constructed constraints - such as social norms - as well as those of the market (such norms are often presented as natural rather than social constraints). But more generally feminist economists tend to reject any single definition of their field, preferring to have it defined by their actual practices and the area on which they concentrate.

## Rational Economic Man

Feminist economists have criticised REM as an erroneous account of human behaviour, and the neo-classical conception of the economy derived from this account as therefore similarly flawed. This models society as made up of autonomous beings guided only by their desire for pleasure, who spring fully formed into existence, complete with exogenously given unchanging preferences. Individual actors do not have any childhood or other period of dependence, nor do they have any dependents. They are assumed to be selfish and to have no impact on each other except through the market. To assume otherwise would be to undermine the theorems of welfare economics that justify neo-classical adherence to laissez-faire policies and market-based solutions to economic problems.

Paula England calls REM a 'separative self', an autonomous individual who can be conceptualised and holds preferences independently of his environment.[7] This conception of the individual leaves no room for the ways in which people are shaped by their life experiences, with their preferences changing as a result. Further, the assumption of selfishness is incompatible with how family and much other life is conducted, and fails to reflect the reality of mutual interdependence that characterises all societies. Indeed behaviour compatible with REM is what would normally be seen as pathological.[8]

---

6. Julie A. Nelson, 'The Study of Choice or the Study of Provisioning? Gender and the Definition of Economics', in *Beyond Economic Man* (see note 6).
7. Paula England, 'Separative and soluble selves: dichotomous thinking in economists', in Marianne A. Ferber and Julie A. Nelson (eds), *Feminist Economics Today*, University of Chicago Press 2003.
8. Irene Van Staveren, *The Values of Economics: An Aristotelian Perspective*, Routledge 2001.

Feminist economists criticise REM as not a good account of either male or female behaviour, and one which specifically ignores the reality of the many ways in which women can have agency in their lives. Women's lives are often centrally involved in the nurturance and care of others, but REM neither needs, nor would he give, care. In that sense much of the androcentrism that invades the whole of economics can be seen as resulting from its reliance on REM, assumptions about whom specifically abstract from the concerns of many women. It is quite appropriate then that rational economic man is unusual among abstract models in having an explicit gender.

## Inside the household

Traditionally the household has been treated in economics as the basic unit of consumption. In the diagram of flows around the economy to be found in nearly every economics textbook, the role of the household is to sell labour, or other factors of production, and to buy consumer goods. This household is taken to act like an individual decision-maker: it is effectively a black box whose members somehow manage to act as if controlled by a single REM, but whose internal workings are outside the domain of economics.

Feminists have made two distinct criticisms of the neo-classical treatment of the household: first, that households have always been sites of production as well as consumption, and second, that a household cannot be treated as a single internally homogenous decision-making unit.

As regards the first point, because much of the domestic and community work that women do is unpaid it is not counted as part of the national product. This is because national accounts, reflecting economic theory, only count services that are marketed. However, as a result of a resolution passed at the World Conference on Women in Beijing in 1995, countries have now been charged with producing satellite national accounts which take account of unpaid work and value it alongside GDP. Many countries have now produced such accounts.[9]

Having such data is important because it makes it possible to assess the effects

---

9. These accounts are called 'satellite' accounts because they do not replace GDP accounting, but augment it by counting in a separate account the contributions of unpaid labour that GDP accounting ignores. The UK's experimental household satellite account uses a particularly innovative approach in attempting to measure the output of the unpaid sector, not just its inputs, as most other countries do. See www.statistics.gov.uk/hhsa/hhsa/Index.html.

of policy changes on the unpaid economy. It can show the mistake of assuming that work within the household is costless and, in particular, that policies that increase such work may be unsustainable. For example, the increasing participation of women in paid work has restricted the supply of relatives and neighbours who can help with child and elder care, and of community volunteers, and - for those involved in subsistence farming - of family members who produce crops for the household.

Ignoring unpaid labour results in the standard economic measures such as GDP misrepresenting the output of the whole economy, both paid and unpaid. It also means

'it is quite appropriate that rational economic man is unusual among abstract models in having an explicit gender'

that growth rates of GDP over- or under-estimate the growth rate of the whole economy, to the extent that there are transfers of production between the paid and unpaid economies. In times when labour is moving from the unpaid to the paid economy, growth rates of GDP overestimate the growth of the whole economy; when there is movement from the paid to the unpaid economies GDP rates understate the growth of the whole economy.[10] Nevertheless, economists and policy-makers continue to target their policies on raising GDP growth rates, despite the distorting effects that concentrating solely on the paid economy can produce.

The second point that feminist economists have made about the household is that it is a site of both conflict and co-operation between members with varying amounts of power. Members of a household cannot be assumed to share equally in its resources, enjoy the same standard of living or be equally well-served by its decisions. Methodologically, there is no reason to assume that a household behaves as a unitary decision-maker. In response to this criticism, mainstream economists have searched for reasons why they can continue in their assumptions. Thus Paul Samuelson claimed that, because 'blood was thicker than water', family members would agree on joint preferences. Gary Becker proposed a justification more in line with the individualism of REM. He

---

10. Barnet Wagman and Nancy Folbre, in 'Household services and economic growth in the United States, 1870-1930', *Feminist Economics*, 2, 1996, show that both types of mistakes have occurred over the past century in the US.

showed mathematically that if one member of a household has sufficiently large an income and is sufficiently altruistic then it is in the interests of all members to behave *as though* they shared this 'head' of household's preferences. What gives the head this power is not only his greater earning power and his altruism, but the assumption that he has the last word. This model, true to the spirit of neo-classical economics, in practice resurrects the assumptions behind the legal framework of Victorian England. Such a head of household has no explicit gender but is clearly assumed to be the paterfamilias.

This model - if it ever applied - has long become outdated, as women have developed the power and the resources to challenge male authority within households. Empirically it has also been falsified, and shown to lead to poor outcomes when applied in development policy. That economists continue to use such a model demonstrates their dependence on the theorems of neo-classical economics, and/or their woeful ignorance of the realities of modern domestic life. An account that assumes that the major contribution to a household is the financial one made by the implicitly male head of household reconfirms the primacy of paid work and results in conclusions that simply validate existing inequalities and support the traditional male breadwinner family. As feminist economists Nancy Folbre and Heidi Hartmann have pointed out, such models also assume that men have a sort of Jekyll and Hyde character, altruistic in the home and selfish in the marketplace.[11]

## Investigating care

The area in which feminist economics has made the most significant positive contribution to economics is in the theorisation and investigation of care.[12] Care is a personal face-to-face service that enables others to have their personal needs met. Everyone needs care when they are young, as do many adults, yet caring responsibilities and caring labour are unequally distributed by gender. Feminist economists are particularly interested in exploring the implications of the way in which care transcends categories of mainstream economics (as noted earlier, self-interested and autonomous REM neither needs nor provides care).

---

11. 'The rhetoric of self-interest and the ideology of gender', in Arjo Klamer et al (eds), *The Consequences of Economic Behaviour*, Cambridge University Press 1988.
12. See, for example, Gabrielle Meagher and Julie Nelson, 'Feminism in the Dismal Science', *The Journal of Political Philosophy*, 12(1).

Care is intriguing because it is both a motivation (relevant to discussion of choice and agency) and an activity (a choice that might be made) that promotes well-being (an output). Care can be seen as a form of work, in that it is purposeful activity that meets needs, takes time and energy and prevents other uses of a person's time, but it is different from other types of work in that the relational context in which it is going on is crucial. Care is therefore not only the provision of a service, but at the same time the development of a relationship.

There has been much criticism of unpaid familial care being held up as the 'natural' form of care, the form against which other kinds of care are to be measured and likely to be found wanting. This approach has led to the skills that make for good care being devalued, because seen as natural feminine characteristics, effortlessly picked up (by women) in the family rather than as purposively acquired skills. But a variety of different types of skills are needed in caring: as well as formal skills, some tacit and particularistic skills are required: how to care for a particular person needs to be learned and such understanding develops through practice. This again becomes something seen as natural, based on blood ties rather than a relationship built up over time.

Carers pay a heavy penalty for assuming caring responsibilities. Unpaid carers have reduced time for earning an income and suffer labour market penalties if they try to combine paid work with caring responsibilities, since rates of pay for part-time work are considerably below those for full-time employment. Paid care attracts low wages and is seen as unskilled. Further, even compared with jobs requiring the same level of formal education and skill, there is a pay penalty for jobs that involve caring. A 1999 review of studies of pay differentials concluded: 'We know of no studies that have used a measure of a concept resembling caring work in an earnings regression and not found a negative effect'.[13]

Feminist economists have stressed the importance of social norms in understanding this phenomenon: gendered norms are important in defining who needs care, how much is needed and above all who should provide it. Norms do change over time but men have not taken up caring at the same rate as that at which women have changed their patterns of work. While care is increasingly

---

13. Paula England and Nancy Folbre, 'The cost of caring', *Annals of the American Academy of Political & Social Science*, 561, 1999, p43.

available on the market, those who most need to purchase care may not be the ones with the resources to do so, especially since women's pay continues to lag significantly behind men's. This begs some questions over the future of care: how much care will be performed and by whom? A growing deficit of care could signal a shift away from what many feminists would see as a woman's view of the norms that characterise a good society towards one in which market norms, traditionally associated with men, come to dominate.

## Gendered processes in the labour market

The standard neo-classical assumption is that differences in pay reflect real differences in productivity, because unfounded discrimination should be competed away. Any employer that paid a man more when a lower paid woman would be equally productive would have higher costs than competitors who did not so discriminate, and so would eventually be bankrupted. On this logic, the gender gap in pay must reflect real differences in productivity. As we have seen, labour market studies have consistently shown that experience, education and occupation explain only part of the difference between men's and women's wages and there remains a persistent unexplained gap. That many labour economists refuse to call this discrimination shows what a strong hold the predictions of neo-classical theory have on economic discourse.

Women's employment histories tend to be more varied and discontinuous than men's. Nevertheless much economics is based on an assumption that employment is full-time and continuous. Women are therefore seen as a special case whose peculiarities have to be explained: men are seen as the normal case, free of the special complicating factors that beset women's employment. Feminist critiques have had a significant impact in this area and few papers these days would fail to attempt to justify (though not always remedy) a concentration on men.

However, there are consequent inadvertent gender biases that remain. For example, skill and occupational classifications are based on male occupations, so there are too few categories for classifying women's occupations, giving the impression of greater homogeneity and lack of progression in skill for women than is likely to be the case.

Women's more varied employment history means that more complex skills and new data sources are needed for its analysis. For example data on family and other caring responsibilities that structure women's labour force participation is needed, but such data is in practice hard to find, not being a standard part of economic data collection.

## Policy

Because feminist economics is a political project, a large proportion of its practitioners are interested in policy. They have analysed the gender implications of a variety of potential and actual policy changes and argued that all policy proposals, whatever their main focus, should be audited for their potential gender impacts.

One reason for this is in order to see how policies are likely to affect existing gender inequalities, so that those that reduce inequalities can be supported and those that worsen inequalities can either be replaced or their gender impact counteracted by other measures. For example, policies that result in cost saving within hospitals may result in patients needing more home care. Without any counteracting policies this may worsen labour market inequalities if women are more likely to take time out from employment to look after sick relatives. However, combined with a home care service and statutory paid emergency leave for carers, the policy may lose its deleterious effects on gender inequalities. Indeed it may improve them, if the home care service then gets used in other circumstances.

Considering the gender impact of policies is also necessary because men and women may respond differently to policies. Where the behavioural impact of a policy is gendered, not to take this into account would result in such policy being badly targeted and ineffective in achieving its goals. To take the above example, if the home care service charges a fee and that fee is above most women's wages, many women will decide not to use it and take time off work instead. This will not only worsen inequalities, it will mean that the home care service is not achieving its goal of reducing interruptions in working patterns. This argument for gender analysis should appeal to all policy-makers, whether or not gender inequalities are the focus of the policies under consideration.

Some overarching critiques of policies have also emerged. For example, policies have been criticised for continuing to be based on a male breadwinner/ female carer household, an increasing outdated model. Policies have also been criticised for colluding with a notion that caring activities are their own reward and that an unequal division of caring responsibilities is simply matter of personal choice rather than symptomatic of a structural problem that needs to be addressed.

In all this feminist economics has had some formal success. Many policy-makers now give lip service to the idea of paying attention to the gendered outcomes of their policies. For example, politicians in the UK are now less likely to treat as a matter of indifference the question of the person to whom money for children is paid in a household, and are likely to be concerned about the effects of their policies on women's employment. However, there has been less success in getting politicians to question long held basic assumptions, for example, that everyone in a household lives at the same standard of living, or to question that having a high GDP growth rate should be the long-term aim of economic policy.

# Labour must die

## Andy Pearmain

*Andy Pearmain argues that it is time to face the fact that the Labour Party is in its death throes, and that euthanasia is now called for.*

I simply don't think that the current Labour leadership understands that its political fate depends on whether or not it can construct a politics, in the next 20 years, which is able to address itself, not to one, but to a diversity of different points of antagonism in society; unifying them, in their differences, within a common project. I don't think they have grasped that Labour's capacity to grow as a political force depends absolutely on its capacity to draw from the popular energies of very different movements; movements outside the party which it did not - could not - set in play, and which it cannot therefore 'administer'.

It retains an entirely bureaucratic conception of politics. If the word doesn't proceed out of the mouths of the Labour leadership, there must be something subversive about it. If politics energises people to develop new demands, that is a sure sign that the natives are getting restless. You must expel or depose a few. You must get back to that fiction, the 'traditional Labour voter': to that pacified, Fabian notion of politics, where the masses hijack the experts into power, and then the experts do something for the masses: later ... much later. The hydraulic conception of politics.

So said Stuart Hall, in 'Gramsci and Us' (see *The Hard Road to Renewal*, Verso 1988, p171), nearly twenty years ago now. New Labour was a response of sorts to that critique, and drew heavily on the late 1980s 'New Times'/*Marxism Today* analyses with which Stuart Hall was himself associated. They did make an attempt at a kind of virtual, heavily mediated connection with some of those emerging social 'movements outside the party'. But many of us now feel that it was a peculiarly selective and distorted response. The de-classed 'identity politics' we contributed to the New Labour project, with its worthy emphasis on race and gender and sexuality and sometimes giddy consumerism, came out the other end as Philip Gould's 'suburban populism' (Gould's 1998*The Unfinished Revolution* 1998 is the urtext of New Labour, a work of shallow genius, laying bare quite unintentionally the project's emotional impulses and social bases). Our disintegrating industrial proletariat was reconstituted as their Home Counties petty bourgeoisie.

It may seem now that 'New Labour is unravelling', but with the prospect of Brownite renewal offering a variant strain, we should remind ourselves that it's still there and in government. Gould and others are insisting that the project's achievements are deep and permanent, in changing the terrain on which their New Tory opponents have to operate and in 'transforming' the Labour Party (albeit effectively out of existence). Whatever, New Labour needs to be historically accounted for, even if it's only so we don't fall for something like it again. It's time to ask - what was New Labour all about? Beneath the bossy spin and the rising, scummy tide of sleaze, what has happened in the fifteen-odd years since New Times?

If we look beyond the glossy rhetoric of ministers and advisers, and the Blair/Brown Punch and Judy show, two particular components of New Labour seem to have come to the fore, squeezing out the far richer mix which the best of late-period *Marxism Today* represented:

♦ An odd kind of shallow, quasi-Marxist determinism, which argues the 'historical inevitability' of capitalist globalisation with exactly the same kind of dogmatic fervour and disregard for politics and ideological conflict, or real human agency of any kind, as marked Second International social democracy and later forms of (mainly Stalinist or Trotskyist) leftism. ('Whoops', I've often found myself thinking in response to Brown or Milburn's latest eulogy to the global market, 'your roots are showing'.) Socialism (or now, globalisation) is coming - all we can or need do is ready ourselves for the new dawn.

♦ A nerdy awe of information technology, characteristic of people who don't really understand its scientific or logical bases and that it's only ever as good as the creative uses that people put it to. This combines, in the writings of

Leadbeater, Mulgan et al, with a taste for way-out and ultimately empty 'new age' management theory to create an approach to government (or should I say 'governance'?) more suited to a millenarian cult than a modern, secular political party. The future is coming. It is bright and shiny. If you don't embrace it you will die ... Prepare for lift-off!

(Alan Finlayson's book, *Making Sense of New Labour* (L&W 2003) is especially good on these features of New Labour, even if - in my view - he understates the continuities of Labourism.)

But is New Labour really that new? It likes to think and insistently tell the rest of us that it is. The project's 'visions' and 'models' are supposedly written on a historical blank sheet. But it incorporates far more old-fashioned, horny-handed Labourism than it cares to admit, even if only because it is grudgingly dependent on the Labour Party electoral machine to 'get out the vote' every few years, and on the likes of John Prescott to keep the North of England in line. And is New Labour's 'technocratic managerialism' really all that different from the 'hydraulic' Fabian expert-ism that Stuart Hall described in 1987? The cumbersome, room-size, calculating machine may have given way to a palm-top computer, but it's still churning out the same old exhortation to 'trust the experts' on everything from macro-economics to public sector reform and so-called 'social exclusion'.

I would argue that, within the history of the Labour Party and the 'broader' democratic left in Britain, New Labour is simply the latest manifestation of Labourism, that inert, stodgy defence-mechanism of a fractious, fissured working class firmly, grimly entrenched within capitalism.[1] For all of its hundred-plus years, it has drawn on the energies of more dynamic but marginal and ephemeral social movements to renew itself and in particular to get its professional cadres re-elected to parliament. That is the real, thoroughly

---

1. I understand, and sympathise with, the argument advanced by Neal Lawson and others that New Labour has inverted the rhetoric of social democracy, moving from the idea of making 'the market fit for people' to that of making 'the people fit for market'. Ultimately, however, this only ever was precisely that, rhetoric, and the achievements of social democracy have been pretty paltry, at least in Britain. The NHS is arguably the only lasting product of labourism, which explains people's deep emotional attachment to it, but even the health service contains deep, intractable flaws, most obviously the residual obstructive power of consultants and GPs, bizarrely reinforced by New Labour. In retrospect, British social democracy was never much more than an intellectual clique. It expired in the 1970s and no amount of wistful re-thinking will bring it back to life.

dispiriting, historical outcome of 'Labour's capacity ... to draw from the popular energies of very different movements *outside* the party'.

The Labour Party was founded on the back of the great upsurge in mass, 'national-popular', democratic activism in late-Victorian, still overwhelmingly industrial Britain. Even then, it managed to combine all sorts of other ideological components from what was at that time an extraordinarily rich 'civil society', such as radical Liberalism and Marxism, Methodism and pacifism, feminism and male chauvinism, imperialism and internationalism, voluntarism and statism, municipalism and parliamentarism - all these and more, in often dynamic contradiction. This was the celebrated (and much admired elsewhere) 'broad church' approach to working-class politics, with deep roots in daily life and about as close as Labour ever came to a genuinely 'hegemonic' strategy for taking and exercising power. Then came Ramsay MacDonald, the first in an almost pathological pattern of 'betrayal' and dashed expectations, which forms the sorry emotional *leitmotif* of Labour history.

The travails of the 1920s and 1930s at least helped to focus and popularise the party, to lay the basis for the post-war heyday of Labourism, and this culminated in the highest ever popular Labour vote in 1951. Even then, there were 'betrayals' and disappointments along the way (Oswald Mosley and his 'New Party', Stafford 'austerity' Cripps and eventually the labourist patron saint Nye Bevan himself). The Labour governments of 1945-51 have gone down in myth as the golden age that ushered in the welfare state and the NHS, but these too were seriously flawed. And of course, though Labour got its highest ever vote in 1951, it lost the general election to the new 'one nation' Conservatives. Labour's subsequent and ambitious attempt at 'technocratic managerialism' under the leadership of Harold Wilson was underpinned and propelled by Crosland's social-democratic 'revisionism' and the corporatism represented by 'beer and sandwiches at number 10' for trade union barons: it foundered on its own internal contradictions amid the capitalist crises of the 1960s and 1970s.

Along the way, there were repeated attempts by Labour to tap into new popular energies, such as the war-time 'Dunkirk spirit' of national togetherness; or the 'scholarship generation' of 1950s working class intellectuals borne along on their parents' hard-won affluence and aspirations; or their younger brothers and sisters ebulliently engaged in the *evenements* of 1968 and after. (I have a particular interest in the latter, as the final example of the 'broad' left attempting a truly hegemonic take on British political economy, via the social contract and the alternative economic strategy in its first, pre-Bennite form. But it swiftly retreated from mass politics into the far more comfortable settings of trade union office, seminar room and 'left-leaning' newspaper columns.)

In the 1980s, Labourism tried several different takes on the 'new social forces', partly derived from 'the politics of identity' which Stuart Hall and others were helping to articulate. Bennism had a go first, with an opening to the non-Labour left of feminists, black and gay activists. This generally ended in tears when they rubbed other, more straight-laced members of 'the broad church' up the wrong way, so to speak. As Thatcher embarked on her full-frontal mid-80s assault on 'loony leftism', we embarked on yet another round of recrimination and disillusionment. The 'soft left' was in part an honest attempt to salvage something from the wreckage. Egged on by Kinnock's 'favourite Marxist' Eric Hobsbawm, and by the Eurocommunists' favourite Labourist Bryan Gould, it came perilously close to a thoughtfully reformist, outward looking and alliance building politics, but at its big soppy heart Labour remained a party of tribalists. All talk of pacts and alliances fell away when they sensed that with professional advertising and media management to gloss up the product, Labour could go it alone just like in 1945. Finally, as we've seen, New Labour took off on its own messianic journey into 'New Times'.

\*\*\*

My analysis is open to challenge on a number of counts. Labour has in its hundred-plus years achieved some genuine amelioration in the living conditions of the industrial working class. Imagine what the last century would have been like if capitalism had been able to exercise the free hand it has now. Unemployment and related benefits, state pensions, some measure of protection against injury and discrimination at work, comprehensive education (even post-war access to grammar schools for bright poor kids like me) and social housing are all real consolations for the miseries inflicted by the 'free market'.

New Labour continues to devise and to offer its own consolations. Just recently I heard one of its advocates argue that the slush-funds of 'local regeneration' and 'social inclusion' represented a further, proud example of Labour providing compensatory 'access to the state' in addressing 'market failure'. Throw money at anything, I would respond, and it will undoubtedly feel better for a while. Ask any lottery winner. But, as is all too obvious now, these schemes and fixes are easily undermined or even swept away when they are judged 'unaffordable'. All the 'new deals' and 'sure starts' will not survive the next serious recession and round of public spending cuts, let alone a New Tory sweep-out. Besides, they have never provided any basis for a real challenge for power, or rather, in Gramsci's much more resonant term, 'hegemony'.

Then there's the historical absence of much else of value in British working class politics. Even Labour's staunchest critics have felt forced to accept that it has historically been 'the mass party of the British working class'. They have usually campaigned for some wider social ferment, which would force the party to adopt 'more progressive policies'. For much of its history, Labour's only semi-serious political rival, the Communist Party of Great Britain, worked to a strategy of 'militant labourism' (for more on this see Geoff Andrews, *New Times and Endgames*, the final volume of L&W's CPGB history). This would (in ways never entirely spelt out) bring along 'a Labour government of a new type'. Even the 1980s critiques of Hall (and of his *Marxism Today* stable-mate Hobsbawm) were aimed (however tetchily) at eventually restoring Labour's political vigour. What is most striking now about the history of the CPGB is just how deferential it was towards Labour, in all its phases and across all its factions, rather than seeking seriously and strategically (like other more effective European communist parties) to displace their labourist rivals or at least force them to develop a coherent social democracy.

There have been, as I've already noted, some genuinely interesting and creative attempts to connect the Labour Party with wider movements and trends in British society, even if they remained isolated and tentative and have almost always resulted in bad feeling all round. And there was always the powerful argument that any political initiative outside of the Labour Party would inevitably end in narrow, shrinking sectarianism and 'being confined to the political wilderness'. There are plenty of generally very depressing examples of this too, including the fate of the CPGB, and thus there is a serious pro-Labour case to answer. Apart from anything else, there are plenty of 'good people' still in and around the Labour Party (many of them clustered around Compass) who would place themselves within our self-styled 'democratic left' but still need persuading that Labour is really and truly dying.

*Labour must die*

I would argue now that, for a whole range of reasons, Labour is no longer the mass party of the British working class, not least because its leadership has decided (understandably) that it doesn't want it to be. This sounds obvious but it needs spelling out, and in historical terms is the primary explanation for Labourism's long decline. The long-term retreat and fragmentation of the working class and the breakdown of its tribal habits and loyalties was one of the primary reasons for the New Labour manoeuvre.[2] Voting and (especially) membership figures attest to the party's decline as an active political (or even social and cultural) presence in the real, everyday world. Hence the reliance by New Labour on 'spin', through a generally compliant or appeased media, as the only remaining means of reaching its 'public'. In a very practical sense the Labour Party barely any longer exists 'on the ground' where most of us spend our daily, increasingly de-politicised, lives.

This surely is the real but barely commented-upon reason for Labour's fawning reliance on money from rich business people, donated or loaned. Labour is simply not receiving enough in membership fees to pay for the operation of a modern, media-dependent political party, let alone enough to make up for dwindling and politically uncomfortable trade union support. The Jowell/Mills and 'loans for peerages' affairs attest to the real sorry organisational state of the party, but the response to them also attests to the residual ethical framework of labourism: a large part of the public revulsion with Labour is made up of scorn for the bosses' ill-gotten gains - how can 'our people' be so cosy with 'them'? That's why nobody's much bothered about the Tories' much greater reliance on handouts from the plutocrats of bandit capitalism, because it's what we expect. New Labour's ultimate failure lies in being unable to shake off the ethical straitjacket of labourism, while the real political agency of the party continues to shrivel.

\*\*\*

So what do we do now? We could usefully revisit one of the central arguments of the first, late-1950s New Left - that Labourism is an obstacle to the wider

---

2. Documented in Hobsbawm's magnificent 'The Forward March of Labour Halted', *Marxism Today* 1978, and since established as part of prevailing political common sense.

social ferment we need in order to bring about progressive change in Britain. The modern democratic impulses at work in Britain, beyond the sterile pantomime of parliament and its regional and local clones, are going on despite not because of Labour. Tribally, instinctively, mythologically, it remains deeply suspicious of Hall's 'movements outside the party which it did not - could not - set in play, and which it cannot therefore administer'. It pains me to say it, but the examples of genuinely democratic developments I am most professionally familiar with from the last twenty years (health and social care for people with HIV/AIDS, for instance, or tenant participation in housing) received far more government support - financial and moral - under the Tories than under Labour.

Thatcherism was a many-faceted beast (and remains so in its 'transformist' adaptations).[3] In its urge to 'roll back the frontiers of the state', it left quite a lot of space for new ways of providing and receiving services, not just in the deregulated private market but also in the remaining, generally battered public sector. It was possible to deploy Thatcherism's anti-statist thrust in some surprisingly creative, invigorating and genuinely innovative ways. We felt 'freer', even if only to harm ourselves and those around us. We could be 'who we really are', even if that ultimately meant being confined to particular, comfortable, sealed boxes of sexual, gender, 'cultural' or ethnic identity, locked in an uneasy stand-off in our supposedly diversifying society. We could choose our lifestyles and circumstances, even if the very exercise of choice consigned others to deeper subordination. We could take pretty much exclusive responsibility for the upbringing of our children, even if it took extraordinary dedication and sacrifice to do it half well, not to mention enough class status and confidence to avoid the 'protective' scrutiny of the moral agents of the soft state. We could purchase anything - any kind of pleasure, our own homes and cars, shares in privatised utilities, high quality education and health care, 'fancy foreign holidays', above all our own social identities - that is, who those around us thought we were.

New Labour of course accepts all this, but in an oddly joyless, fastidious and ultimately begrudging spirit. The 'celebration' of Thatcherism is the aspect of the 'New Times' legacy they bridle most at. New Labour accepted the invitation to the party, but they're still standing in the corner with their ties and belts

---

3. Stuart Hall's writings on Thatcherism remain deeply perceptive and reward repeat reading, notwithstanding many of the subsequent simplifications and caricatures of his work.

done up tight, watching everyone else enjoy themselves. Really and truly, New Labour disapproves of Thatcherism's freedoms, what Stuart Hall has called its license to 'hustle'. It has, by contrast, rushed to accommodate and deepen all the 'regressive' elements of Thatcherite 'modernisation' - globalisation above all, but also its closely related project of 'authoritarian populism'. In its drive to get us all 'ready for market', it shows growing disregard not just for the traditional niceties of the liberal state but for any kind of difference or dissent beyond those officially sanctioned within its own 'respect agenda'.[4] It is even more inclined than in 1987, when Stuart Hall wrote these words, to regard as 'subversive' anything which 'doesn't proceed out of the mouths of the Labour leadership.' And again, why should we be surprised? Personal liberty, in its deeply English (and highly, even globally, attractive) form of comic irreverence and wilful individualism, has always been inimical to the Labourist tradition of dour conformity.

\*\*\*

The problem for the democratic left is that the actual, final death of the Labour Party, as an organisation of people with deep vested interests in its survival, doesn't look like happening any time soon. Labourism as an ideological strand is clearly exhausted but the Labour Party itself has powerful organisational life-support systems, not least the networks of local and national state patronage it still controls. (These range from the allocation of council services to seats in the House of Lords, via allowances for local councillors who would struggle to find anything else worthwhile to do, and the rather more lucrative salaries of MPs and the burgeoning ranks of Assembly members.) The Labour Party simply is, even if it has lost any sense of where it might be going and any historic mission beyond the vacuities of the Third Way. The real question for us then is - what can we do to help kill it off?

There are epochal processes at work within British politics that seriously

---

4. This is where Labourism's shared roots with Fascism become most apparent. I am aware that this is a deeply contentious issue, and that the term 'fascist' is too often deployed for the purposes of what Stuart Hall called 'facile name-calling'. All I would say for now is that serious study of the social and cultural basis of fascism reveals a surprising amount of common ground with socialism and even shared personnel - Mosley and Mussolini being the most obvious examples.

threaten the Labour Party's survival. The decline of popular faith and involvement in electoral politics is eroding its own popular base. Very few local Labour Parties nowadays are capable of a 'total canvass' of their wards, which was always the pre-requisite for the regular, well-oiled Labour ritual of 'getting out the vote'. The party has officially lost more than half its membership since 1997, and that figure does not include the large numbers of people (like my wife) who stopped paying dues years ago but still receive members' mailings and presumably are still counted as members because they never got round to actively resigning. As it loses local council seats, not to mention local 'activists', there are fewer local councillors to do the actual donkey work. The policy/lobby group Compass shows signs of intelligent life, but they are about the only ones around the Labour Party. It remains to be seen how much long-term impact or influence they have.

The decline of interest in electoral and party politics among younger people has been well documented. They are simply not acquiring the habits of 'civic duty' of previous generations. However, that's not to say they are politically uninterested. In my experience of parenting and teaching some of them, I find a hunger for insight and explanation to help make sense of the bewildering world around us. They very often end up looking in the wrong places, embarking on forms of 'political tourism' and returning from their global gap years with the simplistic, unsustainable pieties of 'anti-capitalism'. But they are not in any numbers going anywhere near the Labour Party or anything else which might engage them in the hum-drum but utterly crucial routines of national-popular politics.

We may just at the next election, by a fortuitous combination of luck and tactical design, arrive at a hung Parliament. That's assuming that the imminent deterioration in economic and political circumstances, which have so far spared New Labour any serious test, doesn't deliver something nastier. Then, if the notoriously slippery Lib Dems can hold their nerve and insist on Proportional Representation, we might just see the beginnings of a properly democratic, modern political system, which genuinely reflects the real currents of popular feeling. That would include all those of us on the democratic left who finally, historically, have had enough of Labourism, the Labour Party and all its ways and works.

That's a relatively optimistic short-term view. I don't share it: far more likely is a New Tory Cameron government, sooner or later displaced by some form of neo-Thatcherism - which remains the strongest ideological impulse in Britain. But all of that should be of secondary concern to anyone who wants to see real, deep, meaningfully left-wing transformation of British society in all its cultural, social, political and economic aspects. We need a new political formation, which will survive the demise of the Labour Party, and hopefully play an active, purposeful part in the long overdue historical 'project' of killing it off.

### Postscript for Walter Wolfgang
(the 78-year-old Labour Party member ejected from the 2005 Labour Conference for heckling Jack Straw about the Iraq war)

> 'In June 1934, (Oswald Mosley) was able to stage a great demonstration at Olympia in London, the principal novel features of which were the elaborate spotlighting of the "leader" and the brutal treatment of hecklers.'
> H. Pelling, *The British Communist Party*, A&C Black, London 1958, p83.

# BACK ISSUES

Issue 1 - **Launch Issue** – Andrew Blake, Beatrix Campbell, Barbara Castle, Simon Edge, Stuart Hall, Fred Halliday, Mae-Wan Ho, Heather Hunt, Lynne Murray, Ingrid Pollard, Michael Rustin Lola Young.

Issue 2 - **Law & Justice**, editor Bill Bowring - contributors - Kate Markus, Keir Starmer, Ken Wiwa, Kader Asmal, Mike Mansfield, Jonathan Cooper, Ethan Raup, John Griffith, Keith Ewing, Ruth Lister and Anna Coote. Plus Steven Rose/ Jeffrey Weeks/ David Bell.

Issue 3 - **Heroes & Heroines** - contributors - Barbara Taylor, Jonathan Rutherford, Graham Dawson, Becky Hall, Anna Grimshaw, Simon Edge, Kirsten Notten, Susannah Radstone, Graham Martin and Cynthia Cockburn. Plus Anthony Barnett/ David Donnison/ John Gill and Nick Hallam.

Issue 4 - **The Public Good** - editor Maureen Mackintosh - contributors - Gail Lewis, Francie Lund, Pam Smith, Loretta Loach, John Clarke, Jane Falkingham, Paul Johnson, Will Hutton, Charlie King, Anne Simpson, Brigid Benson, Candy Stokes, Anne Showstack Sassoon, Sarabajaya Kumar, Ann Hudock, Carlo Borzaga and John Stewart. Plus Paul Hirst, Grahame Thompson/ Anne Phillips/ Richard Levins

Issue 5 - **Media Worlds** - editors Bill Schwarz and David Morley - contributors - James Curran, Sarah Benton, Esther Leslie, Angela McRobbie, David Hesmondhalgh, Jonathan Burston, Kevin Robins, Tony Dowmunt and Tim O'Sullivan. Plus Phil Cohen/ Duncan Green/ Cynthia Cockburn.

Issue 6 - **'Young Britain'** - editor Jonathan Rutherford - contributors - Jonathan Keane, Bilkis Malek, Elaine Pennicott, Ian Brinkley, John Healey, Frances O'Grady, Rupa Huq, Michael Kenny and Peter Gartside. Plus Miriam Glucksmann/ Costis Hadjimichalis/ Joanna Moncrieff.

Issue 7 - **States of Africa** - editors Victoria Brittain and Rakiya Omaar - contributors - Basil Davidson/ Augustin Ndahimana Buranga/ Kathurima M'Inoti/ Lucy Hannan/ Jenny Matthews/ Ngugi Wa Mirii/ Kevin Watkins/ Joseph Hanlon/ Laurence Cockcroft/ Joseph Warioba/ Vic Allen and James Motlasi. Plus Bill Schwarz/ Wendy Wheeler/ Dave Featherstone.

Issue 8 - **Active Welfare** - editor Andrew Cooper - contributors - Rachel Hetherington and Helen Morgan/ John Pitts/ Angela Leopold/ Hassan Ezzedine/ Alain Grevot/ Margherita Gobbi/ Angelo Cassin and Monica Savio. Plus Michael Rustin/ Colette Harris/ Patrick Wright.

Issue 9 - **European Left** - editor Martin Peterson - contributors - Branka Likic-Brboric/ Mate Szabo/ Leonadis Donskis/ Peter Weinreich/ Alain Caille/ John Crowley/ Ove Sernhede and Alexandra Alund. Plus Angela McRobbie/ Mario Petrucci/ Philip Arestis and Malcolm Sawyer.

Issue 10 - **Windrush Echoes** - editors Gail Lewis and Lola Young - contributors - Anne Phoenix/ Jackie Kay/ Julia Sudbury/ Femi Franklin/ David Sibley/ Mike Phillips/ Phil Cole/ Bilkis Malek/ Sonia Boyce/ Roshi Naidoo/ Val Wilmer and Stuart Hall. Plus Alan Finlayson/ Richard Moncrieff/ Mario Pianta.

# Back Issues

**Issue 11 - Emotional Labour** - editor Pam Smith - contributors - Stephen Lloyd Smith/ Dympna Casey/ Marjorie Mayo/ Minoo Moallem/ Prue Chamberlayne/ Rosy Martin/ Sue Williams and Gillian Clarke. Plus Andreas Hess/ T. V. Sathyamurthy/ Les Black, Tim Crabbe and John Solomos.

**Issue 12 - Transversal Politics** - editors Cynthia Cockburn and Lynette Hunter - contributors - Nira Yuval-Davis/ Pragna Patel/ Marie Mulholland/ Rebecca O'Rourke/ Gerri Moriarty/ Jane Plastow and Rosie. Plus Bruno Latour/ Gerry Hassan/ Nick Jeffrey.

**Issue 13 - These Sporting Times** - editor Andrew Blake - contributors - Carol Smith/ Simon Cook/ Adam Brown/ Steve Greenfield/ Guy Osborne/ Gemma Bryden/ Steve Hawes/ Alan Tomlinson and Adam Locks. Plus Geoff Andrews/ Fred Halliday/ Nick Henry and Adrian Passmore.

**Issue 14 - One-Dimensional Politics** - editors Wendy Wheeler and Michael Rustin - contributors - Wendy Wheeler/ Michael Rustin/ Dave Byrne/ Gavin Poynter/ Barry Richards and Mario Petrucci. Plus Ann Briggs/ David Renton/ Isaac Balbus/ Laura Dubinsky.

**Issue 15 - States of Mind** - contributors - Alan Shuttleworth/ Andrew Cooper/ Helen Lucey/ Diane Reay/ Richard Graham and Jennifer Wakelyn. Plus Nancy Fraser/ Stephen Wilkinson/ Mike Waite/ Kate Young.

**Issue 16 - Civil Society** - editor Andreas Hess - contributors - Jeffrey C. Alexander/ Robert Fine/ Maria Pia Lara/ William Outhwaite/ Claire Wallace/ Grazyna Kubica-Heller/ Jonathan Freedland. Plus Peter Howells/ G. C.Harcourt/ Emma Satyamurti/ Simon Lewis/ Paulette Goudge/ Tom Wengraf.

**Issue 17 - New Political Directions** - contributors - Sarah Benton/ Giulio Marcon and Mario Pianta/ Massimo Cacciari/ Sue Tibballs/ Richard Minns/ Ian Taylor/ John Calmore/ Judith Rugg and Michele Sedgwick/ Ruby Millington/ Merilyn Moos/ Jon Bloomfield/ Nick Henry/ Phil Hubbard/ Kevin Ward and David Donnison.

**Issue 18 - A Very British Affair** - editor Gerry Hassan - contributors - Gerry Hassan/ Jim McCormick/ Mark Perryman/ Katie Grant/ Cathal McCall/ Charlotte Williams/ Paul Chaney/ John Coakley/ Kevin Howard/ Mary-Ann Stephenson/ David T. Evans. Plus Hilary Wainwright/ Angie Birtill/ Beatrix Campbell/ Jane Foot and Csaba Deak/ Geoff Andrews/ Glyn Ford/ Jane Desmarais.

**Issue 19 - New World Disorder** - contributors Stuart Hall/ Chantal Mouffe/ Gary Younge/ Eli Zaretsky/ David Slater/ Bob Hackett. Plus Jonathan Rutherford/ Anne Costello/ Les Levidow/ Linda McDowell.

**Issue 20 - Regimes of Emotion** - editors Pam Smith and Stephen Lloyd Smith - contributors - Pam Smith/ Steve Smith/ Arlie Russell Hochschild/ Fiona Douglas/ Maria Lorentzon/ Gay Lee/ Del Loewenthal/ David Newbold/ Bridget Towers/ Stuart Nairn/ Rick Rattue/ Nelarine Cornelius/ Ian Robbins/ Marjorie Mayo/ Trudi James. Plus Nira Yuval Davis, Haim Bresheeth, Lena Jayyusi/ Anita Biressi and Heather Nunn/ Andrew Stevens/ John Grieve Smith & G.C. Harcourt/ Fraser Mcdonald & Andy Cumbers.

**Issue 21 - Monsters and Morals** - editor Elizabeth B. Silva - contributors - Elizabeth Silva/ Paul Dosh/ Margrit Shildrick/ Janet Fink/ Dale Southerton/ Caroline Knowles. Plus Geoff Andrews/ Tom Kay/ Richard Minns/ Steve Woodhams.

## Soundings

**Issue 22 - Fears and Hopes** - Irene Bruegel/ Tom Kay/ Paddy Maynes/ Sarah Whatmore and Steve Hinchliffe/ Stuart Hall/ Chantal Mouffe/ Ernesto Laclau/ Geoff Andrews/ Stefan Howald/ David Renton.

**Issue 23 - Who needs history?** - Geoff Andrews/ Kevin Morgan/ Ilaria Favretto/ John Callaghan/ Maud Bracke and Willie Thompson/ plus Michael Rustin/ Ali Ansari/ Costis Hadjimichalis and Ray Hudson/ Christian Wolmar/ Alan Finlayson/ C. Harcourt/ Laura Agustín.

**Issue 24 - A market state?** - Stuart Hall/ Alan Finlayson/ Jonathan Rutherford/ Richard Minns/ Renzio Imbeni/ George Irvin/ Adah Kay/ Nora Räthzel/ Michael Saward/ Nora Carlin/ Michael Rustin.

**Issue 25 - Rocky times** - Geoff Andrews/ Alan Fountain/ Ivor Gaber/ Ash Amin, Doreen Massey, Nigel Thrift/ Gerry Hassan/ Hugh Mackay/ Francisco Domínguez//George Irvin/ Grahame Thompson.

**Issue 26 - Resisting Neo-liberalism** - Katharine Ainger, Geoff Andrews, Cynthia Cockburn, Jane Foot, Stuart Hall, Jeremy Gilbert, Clare Joy, Sayeed Khan, Jo Littler, Ruth Levitas, Doreen Massey, Catherine Needham, Michael Rustin.

**Issue 27 - Public Life** - Sarah Benton, Hilary Cottam, Francisco Domínguez, Alan Fountain, Jonathan Hardy, Neal Lawson, Gregor McLennan, Richard Minns, Geoff Mulgan, Robin Murray, Amir Saeed, Judith Squires, Caroline Thomson, Heather Wakefield.

**Issue 28 - Frontier Markets** - Norman Birnbaum, Alessandra Buonfino, Csaba Deák, Stefan Howald, George Irvin, Richard Johnson, Brendan Martin, Bronwen Morgan, Liz Moor, Chantal Mouffe, David Purdy, Richard Rorty, Judith Rugg, Michael Rustin, Jonathan Rutherford, Michèle Sedgwick.

**Issue 29 - After Identity** - Zygmunt Bauman, Sarah Benton, John Callaghan, Paul Gilroy, John Grahl, Tariq Modood, Steve Munby, Andrew Pearmain, Valerie Walkerdine, Wendy Wheeler, Patrick Wright.

**Issue 30 - Living Well** - Farhad Dalal, John Gittings, Stephan Harrison, Molly Scott Cato, Jacqueline Rose, Michael Rustin, Hetan Shah, Tom Shakespeare, Andrea Westall, Fiona Williams, Ken Worpole, Nira Yuval-Davis.

**Issue 31 - Opportunity Knocks** - Geoff Andrews, Clive Barnett, Sarah Benton, Sally Davison, Lynda Dyson, Sue Gerhardt, Lawrence Grossberg, Lisa Harker, Jo Littler, Martin McIvor, David Purdy, James Robertson, Kate Soper, Rowan Williams.

**Issue 32 - Bare Life** - Pat Devine, Faisal Devji, Kurt Jacobsen, Sayeed Khan, Ruth Lister, Doreen Massey, Richard Minns, Janet Newman, Michael Rustin, Jonathan Rutherford, Ejos Ubiribo, Robin Wilson.

---

All back issues cost £9.99, plus £2 p&p. Order from www.lwbooks.co.uk, or Lawrence & Wishart, 99a Wallis Road, London E9 5LN, or email to soundings@lwbooks.co.uk. Tel 020 8533 2506   Fax 020 8533 7369